Make It Happen!

Linda Pynaker

Make It Happen!
By Linda Pynaker

ISBN: 0-9760933-0-8

First Published August 2004
Second Edition May 2013

Acknowledgments

To my twin sister,
for pouring your heart and creative soul
into painting the cover of
Make It Happen!

To my family and friends,
for growing with me as we develop our souls

To those who contributed their life stories
for the benefit of my readers and myself

To my editor and newfound friend, Steven Manchester;
for his compassion
and incredible attention to detail

Foreword

It's been said that good writers make people think, while great writers make people feel. In *Make It Happen!* Linda Pynaker has proven herself a great writer!

Perhaps it is difficult for me to remain objective, as I am drawn to positive energy and the mysteries of the spiritual realm, but when I read *Make It Happen!* I was literally blown away. With each page turned, I was afforded a rare opportunity to learn how to develop my intuition, eventually enabling me to identify my purpose and discover my life's true path. Using real-life experiences, as well as visualizations and very practical exercises, Linda also taught me the value of creating positive spirals in my life. It didn't take long to prove her theories were right on target. By raising my vibration through enthusiasm, I was able to attract positive things. This resulted in more excitement that attracted even bigger and better opportunities. The payoff: abundance and an overall sense of peace.

Besides being a talented and prolific writer, I have grown to admire Linda Pynaker as a caring and generous human being; one whose life is destined to make an enormously positive impact on society (and at a time when we need it most). Linda devotes herself to helping others as an accomplished psychic medium and healer. She also has a Masters Degree in Social Work and fourteen years experience in family counseling. When put together, her faithful readers get a touch of John Edward, a dash of Sylvia Browne, and the perfect amount of Dr. Phil mixed in.

The direct result of Linda's intuitive gifts and practical experience is the future bestseller, *Make It Happen!* Throughout this spiritual journey, Linda reminds us that every life is inspiring. She also teaches us that we can all make a difference and that we are truly blessed to be here with one another. Although I had great difficulty putting the book down deep into the night, I will caution that *Make It Happen!* can never be finished at a single sitting – it draws you to too many places, within and without, and takes you on too many journeys to ponder and learn from. The lessons, however, have stayed with me long after I finished reading it and I couldn't be any more grateful. I can't imagine a greater gift from any book.

If you're looking for a very practical guide to attract positive opportunities, develop intuition, consider new possibilities and manifest your own destiny, then *Make It Happen!* is the book for you. Containing wisdom of the highest form, its message is still a simple one - that of hope and healing; of living life a little more consciously.

It's been said that luck occurs when preparation meets opportunity. In *Make It Happen!* Linda Pynaker reminds us to be ready for those opportunities by being open to them, prepared and organized. From the best part of my heart, I thank her for that.

Steven Manchester, Best Selling Author of *Twelve Months*

Author's Note

Discovering how to live the life you want to live is an ongoing process, but the more you work toward this goal the easier and more rewarding life becomes.

Many people are dissatisfied with life, and are barely tolerating each day. If this describes you, you know it already. You dread getting up in the morning and sometimes wish you lived somebody else's life.

You are miserable. You dislike your job. Relationships lack meaning or even worse, are demeaning or non-existent. Leisure time is undesirable. There is no joy in life and no hope of life's joy in the near future.

Maybe you have started to improve your life. You have thrown around some ideas and made some important changes in one or two areas, but have yet to figure out what you need to do, so you are still floundering.

If you have already made significant changes and are experiencing success, you are probably hopeful you are on the right track and optimistic that life will become even better than it is now. You are actively working toward your goals and realize it is just a matter of more time and effort before life is wonderful.

Living the life you want to live means feeling fulfilled in all of the areas of life. Contentment and excitement are experienced in the areas that personally mean the most. An overall sense of peace is experienced due to spiritual evolvement and success in overcoming negativity.

If you feel fulfilled, you may decide you do not need to read on or you may continue because your experience is being validated.

If you are miserable, you need to start small. After my divorce when I was only 25 years old, I started by rewarding myself with a muffin. Lying in bed and wishing the world would go away was not an option because I had two small children. Looking forward to a muffin helped me to get through the morning routine and off to work. This is what got me there. The type of reward changed for me over the years, but I did not waiver from my routine. Your reward may be something totally different from a muffin. It might not even be food, but it is essential that you find something to motivate you to start each day.

I no longer need a muffin. This is not an autobiography, so I will not tell you how I progressed from looking forward to a muffin to cherishing special time with family and friends, enjoying my career, appreciating my home, valuing my leisure time, discovering my spirituality, and treasuring my time alone. I hope you will find my ideas helpful and will *Make It Happen!* for yourself.

Contents

Introduction

There is an evolving consciousness about a universal energy from which we all may benefit. People are searching and reaching out. We are discovering that by keeping our vibration high through enthusiasm, positive things are attracted into our lives. When we maintain this enthusiasm, we develop positive spirals in all areas of our lives, as our higher vibration attracts more positive things and leads to even more enthusiasm. This awareness shows us we have greater potential.

We realize that we are not alone. Tapping into our intuition to benefit from the guidance and assistance available from the universe is becoming widespread. There is a growing awareness of synchronicity, those series of seemingly meant-to-be occurrences that happen when we are open. As a result, we are becoming increasingly receptive.

We acknowledge the need to enjoy all aspects of life, with a healthy balance between work, leisure time and relationships with ourselves and others. In our search for abundance and authenticity, we are dissatisfied with superficial conversation and experience a growing need to connect at a deeper level. We are working toward becoming less judgmental and more accepting, leading to an outpouring of unconditional love. Uncomfortable with immersing ourselves in violence and aggression, we want peace. We want spiritual partners—people who support us in our spiritual growth, as we support them in theirs.

Due to people's desire to heal themselves and each other, society is more united. We understand that reaching our full spiritual potential means realizing meaningful connections with ourselves, community and nature's source.

We recognize that each of us is part of a universal energy. Many are able to perceive or see this energy, and facilitate the sharing of energy to heal themselves and others.

It is an exciting time of spiritual growth and enlightenment. It is up to us to *Make It Happen!*

One

Develop Your Spirituality

As I meditated and began to focus upon the reddish orange hue, I could clearly see the mother of my husband at the time.

"You have an important message for me about my book, don't you?"

"Yes."

"What is the message?"

"Write about your own soul development," she said and disappeared.

I was unsure whether I knew what she meant, but I knew my spirit guides would make sure I found out.

I was meditating to try to become clear and was about to give up when a cool ocean breeze wafted across my face. I was indoors, with no open windows or doors and no ventilation system. I knew it was my spirit guides letting me know they were still with me, so I kept trying.

I soon discovered they wanted me to write about how I discovered my ability to heal others through psychic medium readings and sharing healing energy. I had not intended to write about this topic. I wondered whether people were ready, but my writer guides would accept nothing less. They told me, "You have to stick your neck out. Now is the time."

Opportunities to heal others were occurring with increasing frequency. It was both exciting and motivating.

I traveled to my home city, Calgary, and thought the main purpose was to spend some special time with my aging parents and youngest son. I spoke at a large national chain bookstore and endeavored to obtain a media interview to promote the event, but was unsuccessful. It occurred to me that I was meant to do something else with my time there. I was intended to help my family and friends heal through giving them readings.

The next day, my twin sister, Karen, joined me for a few days of my brief stay and was a good sport about visiting my friends and assisting me in giving them free psychic readings.

One of my friends, Yvonne, had recently lost both of her parents and was eager to communicate with them. We agreed to meet her at a restaurant and, after we chatted for a while, Karen and I proceeded with the reading. Yvonne's father appeared when requested. As this was her first attempt to communicate with the other side, Karen was surprised at her ability to receive the messages he sent to pass on to Yvonne. Karen saw a trellis. She asked Yvonne, "Did your father spend time gardening?"

"Only when my mother made him."

"He's telling me that he built a trellis."

"He built a trellis for my mother."

Her mother appeared and told us that she and her husband continued to share tea. My friend later told me that

2

this message, along with knowing that her parents were well, was the most reassuring information she had received from our reading.

She also asked questions about her future. She had interviewed for several employment positions and wondered whether she would get one of them. We identified an intermediate position as assigned to her.

She also asked, "Will I inherit enough money to pay off my house?"

We told her she would receive almost enough money to pay off her mortgage.

The next time I phoned Yvonne, she was just coming in the door from her first day on the new job, confirming our prediction. She also said the inheritance was almost enough to pay off her mortgage. She expressed appreciation toward the hope we gave her and the reassurance she received regarding her parents' wellbeing.

The following day, Karen and I read using extension telephones for a friend who longed to speak to her husband who had passed on several years before. He shared messages for each of their four children and reassured her that he remained present in their lives. He insisted she get on with her life. A couple of weeks later, she told me that although she used to say, "I love you," several times a day aloud or inside her head, she has since thought of him less often. Communication with her husband enabled her to let go and freed her to develop a new relationship.

Karen and I offered to read for our mother. Both of her deceased parents appeared when requested and it was reassuring to her to make contact.

The very next day, we were walking down the sidewalk when a previous co-worker I had not seen in years drove by. We exchanged waves, but she continued to drive down the street. Karen and I picked out a movie at the corner store. As we walked back, we noticed my co-worker driving toward us. She pulled over and explained that she had driven to a house where she was dog sitting only to discover that she did not have the house key with her. When she told us that her ex-husband, with whom she had renewed a friendship had passed on, we offered to visit her the following morning to give her a reading.

Karen and I spoke with her ex-husband and mother, but the information that was most impactful was from her deceased cousin. Both Karen and I saw images of them shopping in a mall, carrying shopping bags and walking almost hand in hand. She confirmed this was their favorite shared activity. Her cousin revealed that she remained in her life and gave examples of things she had observed to reassure her. My co-worker appeared touched to hear that her cousin and best friend remained present in her life.

The reading that struck us most, however, was with one of my dearest friends, Darlene. She had scheduled an appointment with her counselor in Calgary on one of the days she knew I would be in town. It was a five-hour trip each way. Although we were in regular contact by telephone and email, we had not been together in several years. We arranged to meet for lunch. Karen accompanied us and we offered to give Darlene a reading at the restaurant. Darlene's husband, Patrick, had recently passed on in a tragic motor vehicle accident. He immediately joined us when requested.

Once he had provided identifying information, he sent the word *turquoise* and explained that it was water. Darlene had just purchased property on Vancouver Island. Karen, who already lived on the island, told us that there is a lake there the color of turquoise.

Patrick said, "Tell Darlene that when she stands on the shore of the lake and the gentle breeze comes toward her, it is me sending my love to her." This brought tears to our eyes.

He sent another image of the lake, with ripples flowing toward Darlene standing on the shore. He said, "As the ripples flow toward her, that is me sending more love to her." All three of us cried even more.

Our waitress later asked Darlene why we had all been crying and she answered, "My friends were reading and healing me." I felt blessed to be able to provide this for a special friend.

I talked with my mother about communicating with spirits. Though my father pretended to be reading, I knew he was listening. I reassured them that, at the time of their passing, they would be met by their loved ones who had already passed on.

In addition to spending special time with family, my sister and I discovered the power of healing through communicating with those who have passed on.

Shortly after my return to San Diego, a chain of synchronistic events almost immediately followed. I was trying to decide whether to have my hair cut a few days before a speaking engagement. I called the hair salon to find out whether my hairdresser, Maria, was available that day. It was supposed to be her day off, but Maria told me she would be at the salon for awhile, as she had been called in last minute to cover for one of the other hairdressers. I immediately drove there and, for the first time, we were the only two people in the salon. Maria had cut my hair dozens of times and I had never previously mentioned my intuitive abilities, but on this occasion, I did.

Maria asked if I could communicate with her mother who had passed on when she was only three years old. When I asked intuitively whether I should offer to read her immediately, I knew we would be interrupted. A man soon entered the salon and requested a haircut. The hairdresser Maria was covering for arrived as she was finishing my haircut, which enabled Maria to leave. I gave her a reading. It was a touching reunion and I was glad the sequence of events enabled me to help her connect with her mother.

When I returned to the salon the following month, Maria was excited. As indicated by her mother during the reading, she was moving things to demonstrate her presence. Maria also liked knowing that her mother was standing behind her when she was in front of the mirror, as this was something her mother had shared during the reading. Maria would soon be having surgery and she told me it was a relief to know she would not be alone.

She spoke with her adult daughter, who told her that her grandmother has been with her as long as she can remember. Her grandmother strokes her hair and touches her shoulder. She can also see her. When Maria asked her daughter why she never previously said anything, she said she thought nobody would believe her.

Only a few days later, an acquaintance gave me the name and phone number of a woman who wanted me to call because we both share healing energy. I left a message on her answering machine, but did not receive a reply. My impression during the week was that I should call her on Sunday afternoon, so I did.

She lived nearby and we agreed she would come to my home. I immediately received a message that I should light some candles. There was somebody on the other side who wanted to talk to her. As I greeted her at the gate, her father told me he was the one who wanted to communicate with her.

She wanted to know whether I could provide a reading to somebody who was skeptical. Although I should have seen this as a warning, I reassured her that I could.

I asked her father for identifying information. He said he used to enjoy reading the newspaper.

"Yes, sort of."

He had a white car he loved.

"He had a white car, but I didn't know he loved it."

"He did not like to garden."

"Mom did the gardening."

"He liked to watch the news on television."

"Yes, but he couldn't see the TV very well toward the end."

"He died of heart problems."

"Yes, he had diabetes, but his heart was the overall reason."

He sent her love. She wanted to know what to do with the rest of her life and started to cry. She said she blamed her husband for her father's death.

I said, "Let's ask your father."

"I'm not sure it's him," she said.

"What do you need to ask him, so you can be sure?"

She wanted me to ask what his face looked like when he passed on. Her father told me his face was contorted.

"Yes, ask him why."

According to her father, they "pulled the plug" on him.

"Yes, they took away his oxygen." She was unsure about this decision.

Her father communicated that it was his time to go.

She wondered where she should live, asking again what she should do with her life and where she should live. When I looked at a map in my mind, the outskirts of Scottsdale, Arizona looked bright for her. Her father said she should use her hands due to their healing abilities. She acknowledged that she'd often healed others with her hands. He told me she was artistic and had painted beautiful landscapes, and she should do that. She said she used to paint landscapes, but had not painted in a long time.

I hope she will be successful in using this communication to create positive spirals in her life. We can let negative spirals develop where situations move from bad to worse, or choose to maintain enthusiasm to raise our vibration and invite positive things into our lives. This creates positive spirals where our higher vibration attracts opportunities, which creates more enthusiasm, raises our vibration and attracts more opportunities. The main purpose of this book is to assist you in creating as many positive spirals as possible in your life.

When you create a life of positive spirals,
you will vibrate at a level that brings opportunities your way.

Optimism, excitement and laughter are all magnetic qualities that attract opportunities. If you maintain a high vibration, you will be amazed by your achievements. Positive spirals are infectious and also encourage people to respond more positively to you.

A few days after this reading, I received a phone call from an acquaintance who suffered from fibromyalgia, a painful muscle condition. Many healers believe that, although triggered by a physical trauma, the condition is symptomatic of past hurt stored in the muscles. The pain is partially stress related. Though related to storing past hurt, it is usually initiated by a physical trauma and the outcome is physical. It is counterproductive to treat only one or the other.

She said she was calling for writing advice, but I received a message that I should light candles. There was a message for her from the other side. She agreed to a reading over the telephone when I told her that her deceased father wished to communicate with her. I summoned her father and he immediately appeared. He said he loved to read the newspaper and showed himself dressed in casual shirt, tan pants and brown belt, which she confirmed he typically wore at home when working outside.

His alcoholism and abusive behavior created a strain in the family, but she felt they shared a special bond.

As he shared a heartfelt apology, she cried, saying, "I forgive you, Daddy."

My left hand was held straight up like a stop signal and was pulsing back and forth. I received a message that she was releasing past emotional issues and would experience more pain during the next three days, but would soon notice improvement in her health. I had helped her to heal and release energy. Four days later, she emailed me and mentioned that she was feeling better than she had in a long time. She could not stop thinking about the reading and was sure it was her father because of his attire and comment about reading the newspaper. He apparently had risen every morning without fail at 4:30 a.m. to enjoy the newspaper and a cup of coffee.

Only two days later, I was editing one of the chapters of my book. I wanted one straight read through, but was interrupted by a telephone call. Upon termination of the call, my spirit guides told me I should resume editing the chapter. Once I had moved only one paragraph to the beginning of the chapter, I received a message that I should go down to the jacuzzi in my apartment complex. *Very strange.* The next message was that I should provide a reading to a man, Bill, who was already in the jacuzzi. I had read for him once six months previously. Bill had expressed skepticism of psychic abilities and was surprised when I summoned both his deceased grandmother and father, and gave him specific information.

I changed into my swimsuit and started to pour a glass of water, but I received a message that I should wait to get water. *Hurry*. Bill's father had a message for him.

I was receiving messages to *hurry, hurry, hurry*. When I arrived at the jacuzzi, Bill had already covered the jacuzzi and was opening the gate to leave.

"You have to stay. Your father wants to speak to you," I blurted.

He looked at me as though I was crazy.

"I know he's passed on, but remember me, I'm a medium. He really wants to talk to you."

Bill's father was communicating so fast I could hardly understand him. My stomach was churning, as I intuitively sensed his anxiety. I finally picked up that he wanted to provide a warning for somebody at Bill's place of employment. He was adamant that a male co-worker would experience a heart attack, if he did not see a doctor about taking cholesterol medication to get his levels down. *Soon!* He told me the man was in his early 30's, with dark brown hair. When he provided his name, Bill knew him. He had dark brown hair, but he was in his early 40's. I asked his father whether he could be in his early 40's. *Yes.* His father said the man thought he was fit, but he was not. Bill told me the man appeared fit. His father said that the man had a family, a wife and two children, which Bill confirmed. Despite his father's insistence regarding the importance of his message, Bill wondered how he could approach the man at work. His father suggested he say he had a crazy neighbor who had given him the message.

Bill later told me that the man in danger was his employer. He did not feel comfortable about approaching him, so I called instead. His employer was receptive, said he

10

appreciated my call and indicated he would immediately schedule an appointment with his physician.

Only a few days later, I started to respond to an email sent to me by Joan, one of my friends in Calgary. As soon as my hands touched the keyboard, a voice pleaded with me to convince Joan to give him the chance to apologize for his abusive behavior toward her. It was Joan's father. She was not yet aware of my intuitive abilities, but I sent her an email asking her to call me, so I could help her father speak to her.

After providing identifying information and once Joan said she was confident it was her father, he cried and apologized. He said nothing could excuse his behavior and she had not deserved the abuse.

We were also joined by Joan's deceased mother. She indicated that she keeps an eye on Joan and related an incident where she had been present when Joan purchased a silver necklace. Joan asked her opinion about how her brother and sister are doing. Her mother blamed herself for tolerating her father's abuse and not being a better role model for her children, as Joan's siblings are both in difficult relationships. Joan's father slipped his arm around her mother and said he blamed himself; it was not her fault.

Joan inquired about another sister. I got that there was not one here, so I asked her mother if she was with her. *No.* Just as Joan indicated that this sister had passed on in infancy, her mother commented that her third daughter had almost immediately gone into another life and is living in Saskatchewan. Joan's mother said that, unlike her other two daughters who are blonde, this one has brown hair and had grown up on a farm with three siblings. Joan's mother indicated she occasionally checks on her.

Joan asked whether her daughter would have children and I told her she would be expecting within a year. I said her daughter had contracts with three baby beings and would have two children, possibly three depending on what she decided. The first two would be female and if she proceeded with another pregnancy, the third would be a male. I explained that, prior to assuming physical bodies, we may contract with spirit beings to bring them into this world. We may choose to fulfill all or only some of these contracts. Joan advised me that her daughter would like to have three or four children, though her husband only wanted two.

Joan asked whether she should retire and both parents indicated that they thought she was ready. When she asked what she should do, her mother said, "Paint." Her mother showed an image of large blossoms, almost like apple blossoms; they were light pink, almost white, with pink tinged edges. Joan instantly knew the name of the flower and said they were her mother's favorite. Her mother said she would paint them. Joan laughed when I told her that her father showed an image of her in a lounge chair at the beach, with drink at her side and an open book face down at her side, as this was her typical behavior.

Afterwards, Joan told me she always thought she would never want to see her father on the other side. During the previous week, however, she decided it would be acceptable. It is more than coincidence that her father almost immediately asked to communicate with her. She later wrote and told me it was comforting to connect with her parents and hear them apologize. She had always known her mother was with her. When she relayed this information to her sister, she apparently wanted to know whether they also apologized to her. I suggested she give her sister my telephone number. A couple of months later, Joan wrote to say that her daughter was expecting a child. She has since given birth to a daughter.

A friend of the family whom I had never met had recently separated from his wife. She told me that he wondered where he was going to live and where he would work. I told

12

her he would move to Calgary. I saw a vision of a three-story office building with lots of windows on 12th Avenue SW in Calgary and I said he would be working on the third floor. I could see drafting tables, which symbolized him working for an architecture firm.

I said he would be moving to Calgary in August. He would purchase a house in the Shawnessy area and would live near Fish Creek Park.

I could see his dog bounding in the snow in the back yard of his new home and it was surrounded by a chain link fence. There was a park across the street.

I saw him hiking in the mountains with his dog.

I said he would marry a woman with shoulder-length brown hair.

She shared this information, providing him with hope and reassurance. I later found out that everything came to be.

My life purpose is to help people heal, whether I reach them through writing, lectures, spiritual readings or sending healing energy. I am also intended to help people discover their own intuitive abilities.

I did not always know I had these skills. The route for discovering my purpose has been intriguing.

At one time in my life, my goal was to accomplish a cross-country paragliding flight from Golden, British Columbia to Harrogate. Following achievement of this goal, I felt aimless. My husband and I moved to San Diego immediately afterwards and I did not yet have any meaningful relationships in San Diego. Most of my friends and family lived in Canada. I was thrown into an identity crisis, as I tried to figure out what to do with respect to career, relationships and leisure time.

I experimented with a few courses, but nothing appealed to me.

I met a Reiki Master at one of the courses and he later shared healing energy with me. It was an incredible experience. In addition to reaching an altered state of consciousness and seeing a fascinating light show of colors in my mind, I saw visions of myself as a little girl with long blonde hair in a past life. I also saw an image of his Native American Master Guide in buckskins and full headdress.

For several years, Karen had talked about healing energy. I asked her to teach me a few techniques. Several of my neighbors were willing to let me experiment. When sharing healing energy, I again saw colors in my mind.

One of my neighbors had a brain tumor. Sharing healing energy reduced her headaches.

A 69-year-old neighbor broke his clavicle and bruised his entire right side when his bicycle hit a boulder and he tumbled over the handlebars. Despite his pain, he was astonished that he was able to sleep when I shared healing energy with him.

I was driving in my car one day and noticed a huge dog dragging behind her owner, as they walked down the street. I offered to share healing energy with her. She was vibrating with pain and I wanted to give her some relief. She stood quietly and eventually lied down, while I shared healing energy. Her owner told me she was a 19-year-old wolf. As I drove away, she walked four to five times the pace she had before receiving healing energy.

On another occasion, my friend and I stopped to pet a young boxer dog on the lawn. When we turned to leave, he became excited and fell off of a retaining wall. He pulled up one of his hind legs and began limping around on three feet. I asked the owner if I could share healing energy with his dog, but he was reluctant. The dog apparently suffered from hip dysplasia, but he eventually agreed. After receiving healing energy, the boxer returned to bounding around on all four legs.

I would often share healing energy with my co-workers and some of them also saw colors. We would share the colors we were viewing with each other and the hues would almost always match. I began to notice that whenever I closed my eyes, I could see colors. I showed my husband, at the time, how to share healing energy and, when his hands raked through my aura, I could see shafts of light where each one of his fingers separated the energy. I soon noticed that whenever I washed my hair, I could see my own fingers separating the colors of my aura.

The next significant change was that I began reading Stephen King's *On Writing* during my work breaks. For months, the book stood face out on a shelf near my desk and I finally picked it up. It motivated me to begin writing my first book, *Time To Heal*. I was a counselor for fourteen years and, although I did not want to resume my career as a counselor, I still wanted to reach people. I decided to write a book about a woman who rebuilds her life and, in this way, model to women the importance of self-discovery and living the lives they want to live.

A few days later, when I attended a psychic fair, one of the clairvoyants taught me a brief grounding ritual. She suggested I wear blue to help me express my creative side. I grounded myself each time before I sat down to write and enjoyed closing my eyes due to the magnificent display of colors I would see. It became so fascinating that this led me to sit for longer periods of time until I reached a meditative state.

I wrote *Time To Heal* in less than six months, even though I was working full time, and subsequently told an intuitive that I did not think I had written the book alone. She told me that my deceased maternal grandmother had helped me. I continued to share healing energy whenever the opportunity arose. I eventually asked my twin sister what she thought my seeing colors meant.

She said, "Maybe you are going to become a spirit medium."

At the time, I thought this was an unusual response and am now convinced these words were channeled to her.

I had previously experienced several intuitive insights. The first one I clearly remember was when I was ten years old. My mother and grandmother had taken us on a vacation. They were lost in a strange city and were trying to decide which direction to travel. Although I repeatedly showed them which direction was north, they waved me away and told me I did not know what I was talking about. I knew which direction was north and there was no doubt in my mind. I believe this was when I first decided to ignore my clairvoyant abilities, as my family did not take them seriously.

One day, when we were twelve, Karen and I were babysitting together. She returned home, so my father could change the bandage on an infected sore on her hand. A short while after she left, I got up from the couch like an automaton and marched soldier-like to the telephone, with knees high and hands swinging back and forth at my sides. I meanwhile asked myself, *Where are you going? What are you doing?* I walked to the telephone and called home, even though I did not realize this was the number I was dialing.

"What happened to Karen?" was my immediate question when my father answered the phone.

"If you let me hang up the phone, I'll pick her up off the floor," he replied.

She had fainted. He had one hand on her elbow and she slid to the floor, as he reached for the phone with his other hand. It was as if I had been taken over. The experience was so moving that I vomited after I hung up the telephone.

During adulthood, my clairvoyant abilities were often linked to pregnancies. One of my co-workers had decided to become a surrogate mother, as a gift of love to her sister and brother-in-law. One day, I walked into her office space and instantly knew their attempts at artificial insemination had been successful. She announced the next day that she was pregnant.

At another time, I was expecting my second child and was in the beginning hours of labor. At 1:45 a.m., I told my previous husband that one of the women I had met in the obstetrician's office that day had had a baby boy, but by Caesarian section.

He said, "Go back to sleep. You're dreaming."

I knew I was awake. I went into the hospital the next morning to deliver my second son. When my obstetrician arrived, I asked him if that woman had come into the hospital to have her baby.

"Yes, she delivered a baby boy at 1:45 a.m. by C-section," he said.

One of my friends, Valerie, and I both had sons and were hoping our second babies would be girls. Shortly after our second son was born, my first husband and I were driving down the highway on our way home from a visit with one of my sisters who lived out of town.

All of a sudden, I exclaimed aloud and he said, "What?" I told him Valerie had just had a baby girl. He thought I was being silly. When we reached home, the telephone was ringing as we came through the door. It was one of my other sisters calling to say that Valerie had given birth to a baby girl.

After I finished my Masters Degree, I picked up an Employment Bulletin and knew right away that my next employment position was in it. When I decided to leave that job, I picked up a newspaper and knew that my next job was inside. I opened the newspaper to the correct page and noticed the ad.

Months later, my children were chatting about registering for the next soccer season. I startled them both and myself when I said, "We won't be here. We're going back to Calgary. I'll be getting a job at Alberta Children's Hospital in the third week of July." I hadn't yet applied for a job, but I was so certain about this that I began packing our belongings. I was called a few weeks later about a job possibility at Alberta Children's Hospital in Calgary and began working there on July 18th.

During my eldest son's adolescence, my son and his friends frequently drove 75 miles to the Banff area to downhill ski. On one such afternoon, I was driving home from a neighboring town. I had a strong feeling that my eldest son was in danger. I did not have a cell phone and there were no public phones available until I reached Calgary. I stopped at a video store as soon as I reached Calgary and called home from the store. My youngest son told me that his brother was not yet home, but that he had talked to him on the phone and everything was fine. I drove home and, for the first time in my life, paced the floor until my eldest returned.

As they stood outside, I greeted he and his friends at the door looked them over from head to toe and said, "I'm sure glad you're all okay."

After they came inside, they told me they had hit a patch of ice on the highway and their van had turned over in a ditch. Fortunately, nobody was injured. They expressed relief that they had put their skis and snowboards under the seats, so they had not moved around in the van. The driver's father had met them at the side of the road and helped to rescue the vehicle. Because he had not wanted me to worry needlessly, my youngest son had not advised me of the accident at the time of my call.

Following my sister's comment that I might become a spirit medium, I enrolled in a six-month Clairvoyant Training course. During my first practice readings, although I only received the occasional word, at times, I could always see colors. Intuitively asking what they meant often gave me more information. As my experience grew, I started to see detailed colorful pictures, particularly when it related to past lives. Where I excelled, though, was in talking to human and animal spirits.

When I asked my instructor how my grandmother might have helped me write, she said my grandmother put thoughts in my head, but she told me that my grandmother was not the only spirit helping me. There were two and they were standing behind me. That piqued my curiosity.

While I was meditating the next day, two spirits dressed in peacock blue blouses and seated side-by-side in chairs appeared before me. One was my maternal grandmother dressed in a pleated blue blouse she had worn in a photo I have and the other was my husband's grandmother dressed in the blue blouse she had worn in the photo on her memorial service pamphlet. I had not even met my husband until after my grandmother had passed. *How did the two grandmothers get together?* I was later told they were introduced on the astral plane.

When I was asked to talk to a classmate's deceased pet lizard, I thought the idea was ridiculous until I actually received messages. That surprised me.

I later read for Rob, my husband at the time, so he could talk to his deceased mother and grandmother. We then decided I would summon our pet dog, Mandy, who had recently passed on. I told Rob I would put her in a bubble on the left of him.

All of a sudden, he whispered, "Honey, she's on my lap."

We both laughed and said together, "She never did like to do as she was told."

After that, I wanted to spend as much time as possible communicating with spirits. I offered to read for anyone possible and often practiced reading people long distance over the phone.

I eventually discovered that even when I was not intending to do a reading, information would come to me while I was sharing healing energy. I wanted my parents to embrace the idea that we could communicate with spirits on the other side and I sent the following message in a letter to them:

Sometimes people who have passed on show up without me asking them to. I was sharing healing energy with Barbara, a woman who fell down almost an entire flight of ceramic tile stairs at work a few weeks ago. She was bruised and scraped, but astoundingly was not seriously injured. Her common-law husband, Richard, who had passed on, started talking to me.

He talked about two little girls he loved who were "like nieces." Barbara told me the girls were her best friend's daughters. Richard told us that one of them should visit a doctor. When she gasped at this news, he immediately reassured us that it was nothing serious. The girl was experiencing heart palpitations related to anxiety and he thought a physician might be able to help. Richard also said that the reason Barbara hadn't been more injured from her fall was because he had grabbed her arm. She told me that she felt somebody grab her arm, but when she looked around there was nobody there.

He laughed and said, "It was no easy feat, either." Apparently, he had heard her telling a co-worker and myself that she hit the floor hard because she wasn't a featherweight. Richard then sent her so much love that it brought tears to our eyes.

At another time, I sent my parents the following information about my maternal grandparents who had passed on:

Nana and Grandpa visited me last Saturday when I was with one of my friends. She saw them first and asked me who they were. Grandpa is apparently helping me write Make It Happen! Grandpa looked great and had brown hair and a brown mustache. Auntie Eleanor came right behind him. I can hardly believe that I didn't even believe in this stuff a year ago. But I have to now. It is so amazing and very healing for people when they get to talk to people who have passed on.

Last year, a psychic told me that I was going to be more famous than I could handle and that people would come from all over the world to me for answers. I wonder if this is the reason because I can't think of anything else I know that people would come from all over the world to ask me about.

When my mother became extremely ill, I wrote to my parents again:

Mom, Grandpa also says he's watching over you right now and I don't know whether this is comforting, but he says he is looking forward to you joining him on the other side some day. He said that he, Nana and Auntie Eleanor would all be there to help you pass to the other side when the time comes.

The following story is about a woman beckoning her daughter to join her on the other side:

A Moment of Beckoning

In the middle of night, during the fifth month of pregnancy with my fourth child, I began to hemorrhage and it was as if someone had turned on a faucet inside me. The nurses seemed near panic and phoned for the doctor. My doctor was one-half hour away. His assistant came and ushered me into the operating room.

In a haze of semi-consciousness, I remember a nurse saying, "I've never seen anyone bleed like this."

I received four transfusions that night and was later told that I was near death. I remember vividly that I was in a place that had a long corridor and at the end of it a bright light drew me. I walked toward it. Suddenly, my mother, who had passed on eight years prior, appeared and reached out to me. "Lillian," she entreated, "come with me."

I wanted to go with her, but something pulled me back. "Not yet, not yet," I said. I had the feeling that there was much that I had yet to do and I was not ready for death.

I spent the ensuing months in a terrible depression over the loss of the child and I struggled to regain my physical health, but the memory of that incident remains with me, just as vividly as when it happened.

I know that my mother will be there to greet me when I pass.

Lillian Fisher
Alpine, CA

This story reveals a man's message to his granddaughter, as he made his way to the other side:

Goodbye Request

When I was eight years old, my grandfather woke me in the middle of the night. He sat at the foot of my bed, looking as real as anybody. He apologized, asked that I forgive him for sexually molesting me and said he could not go to Heaven unless I forgave him.

I said, "Yeah, sure," and instantly forgave him.

My grandfather said he had died. I started screaming for him not to leave me. He said he had to go, but he would always watch over me because he had a lot more to learn.

My mother came into my bedroom when she heard my screams and told me I was having a bad dream, but I knew I was awake. Just then, the phone rang. It was my grandmother calling from Oceanside to say that my grandfather had died of a heart attack in his sleep.

Anonymous
El Cajon, California

His acknowledgement and apology for his behavior enabled her to heal. Her forgiveness also facilitating healing and enabled him to go to the light. He otherwise might have chosen darkness, because he might not have believed he deserved to go to the light.

Once, when Karen and I were in Calgary together, we stopped by for a brief visit with a couple, Don and Rose, who had been wonderful mentors during our adolescent years. It was great to be able to connect with them.

Don had developed a rare painful condition following a kidney transplant. We visited with Rose for a while and then Don joined us. Karen and I offered to share healing energy with him. He was unable to sit, so he leaned against the back door. As Karen scanned his body, she noticed energy blockage at his heart. I received an intuitive message that this block was related to a childhood issue when he was seven years old. Don revealed that his brother had passed on at that time. I received a message that his mother had been embarrassed by his behavior and he had felt ashamed. He explained that he was running around and being noisy at the memorial service.

I reassured him, "Of course, at that age you would not have realized the permanence of death and your behavior would have been inappropriate." Karen continued to share healing energy, as I spoke.

I asked his permission to summon his mother who had passed on. She provided identifying information. She then told him she loved him and apologized profusely for not having been more understanding. Don's body shook, as he cried without a sound.

His mother said, "It will take a while, but you are going to be okay." Don and Rose revealed that they had just had an unexpected encounter with a medical expert they trusted who had reassured them he would take care of Don.

Don's mother said she is always with him and, to lighten things up, she chuckled, "I've seen what you and Rose have been doing in the bathroom."

Don said, "Rose must have told her!" and everybody laughed.

We exchanged loving embraces before we departed and were glad to have shared such a meaningful encounter.

Animals can be very available for intuitive readings. Karen telephoned and asked if I would see what was going on with one of her daughter's horses, Whimsical. I read that Whimsical was excited about having a baby. I did not realize she was pregnant at the time, but even if I had received that message I would have ignored it. Karen advised me that a stallion had gotten out of his paddock and they had administered injections to the young mares to terminate pregnancies, Whimsical included. She was too young. But, the medication was unsuccessful and Whimsical was pregnant.

A few days later, I received an intuitive message that Whimsical was extremely anxious about giving birth and did not want to be alone. I told Karen that Whimsical would give birth to a foal in one and one-half weeks between the Tuesday evening and Wednesday morning. I got that Karen's daughter would be with Whimsical, as there would be signs of the impending delivery. Even though her mother was a bay, the foal would be chestnut color with a star on the forehead. It looked like there would be a problem, but not with the foal's health.

A chestnut foal with a star on its forehead was born on the predicted Tuesday evening around 9:00 p.m. She was healthy and they named her Extra. Whimsical rejected the foal, however, and would not let her suckle. Karen called and asked me to check with Whimsical to see what was going on. I read that because Whimsical had nearly died from colic when she was a foal, the painful cramps that occurred whenever Extra tried to suckle made her fear for her own life.

When Whimsical's mother, Maplestreet, was introduced to Extra, she snuffled every inch of her body, as if she were her own and immediately assumed the role of mother. Maplestreet was proud and filled with love. She told me that she was very happy and the foal was all she had ever wanted. Karen's daughter manually withdrew colostrum to feed Extra and let her stay with Maplestreet.

After a few days, they were able to trailer in a brood mare and they put Maplestreet into another paddock. Karen called for a reading when this mare also refused to feed the foal. When I checked to see what was happening, the brood mare said she already had a baby and did not know why she needed another one. I got that Maplestreet was repeatedly telling the mare to go home and get away from her baby. Maplestreet told me that she would not be quiet until she returned to Extra. Karen confirmed that Maplestreet had not quit neighing since the other mare's arrival. They eventually returned the mare to her home, reunited Maplestreet and Extra and subsequently fed her goat's milk and foal starter. Extra soon became healthy and rambunctious.

I continued to meditate on a daily basis and the two grandmothers faithfully appeared in their blue blouses seated in chairs in front of me each day. At one point, my grandmother wagged her finger at me and told me that I worried too much. She told me I need not worry, as she was helping me to promote *Time To Heal*. Months later, my grandmother informed me that I no longer needed her and that she would not be at my side, but that if I really wanted to talk to her, I could ask for her.

Time spent meditating became very valuable. I was often aware of astral traveling and I could see myself in the future, speaking publicly or being interviewed on television. It helped me to remain hopeful when I received rejection to many of my requests for media interviews.

At one point, I was aware of looking down at myself in an arena filled with hundreds of people. It was like fast motion. People kept popping out and being replaced by other people.

I asked, "They came to listen to me, didn't they?"

Yes. If ever I doubted that I was going to have an impact on people, that reassured me. It also scared me. But, I know that I do not do this alone. There is a whole team in the spirit world working with me and I know that the universe will support me in the plans for my future.

There was an angel on my bedroom ceiling one morning and he told me his name is Ezekial. We all have many angels assigned to help and protect us.

On another morning when I awoke feeling disheartened and began to meditate, two or three lit up angels whistled by carrying trumpets and horns. They said, "You are not alone. We will help you. We will announce you." Then another one came by playing uplifting music on a horn to reinforce the message. Just seeing angels cheers me, never mind the encouraging messages they send.

One of my spirit guides suggested I replace my Betta fish that had passed on. Sharing our lives with pets is one of the ways we receive love from angels.

I began writing *Make It Happen!* and, as mentioned, my maternal grandfather who had passed on let me know he was assisting me. I eventually realized there was someone else, too, but did not know who it was and did not receive an answer when I asked my grandfather. One day, when I was meditating, two seated people appeared before me just like the two grandmothers. One was my grandfather. I wondered about the two chairs and I soon knew it was a message to help me figure out who the other person was. The grandmother of my husband at the time was the other spirit assisting me. She told me she had been helping me since I had started the first book.

My grandmother had previously spoken for Rob's grandmother, while I was promoting *Time To Heal,* and my grandfather had spoken for her while I was writing *Make It Happen!* She subsequently began speaking to me herself.

Only a few days later, another spirit writer, John, revealed himself to me. He said he joined the team to provide more male energy to the project. He also told me he provided a calming influence due to the anxiety I experienced since being instructed to write about my own soul development.

At one time, I was unsure of my spiritual beliefs. Learning about healing energy opened my mind. Discovering my intuitive abilities cinched it. We each have talents and gifts to help us fulfill our purpose. Your spiritual belief system is the foundation of your life.

The spirits with whom I have communicated have nothing but positive reports about life on the other side. This does not mean I am impatient to join them, or that I will not miss my loved ones when they pass on. But, it is comforting to know they are going to a magical place and I will be able to continue to communicate with them afterwards.

Many of us grew up with organized religion and many attended a church, synagogue, temple or mosque on a regular basis. Some continue to practice this form of worship, some are considering returning and some are choosing other methods of developing their spirituality. Religion is a personal decision and, like anything else, it is important that you pursue whatever avenues are the best personal fit for you.

If your spiritual belief system is something you want to develop, you may read, join a chat line or participate in an organization with people who share similar beliefs. There are many places of worship that specialize in eclectic spirituality.

Developing your spirituality may include
simply taking time to enjoy nature, beauty
and the peacefulness of the outdoors.

There is nothing like nature to get us in touch with our roots, the universe and the wonders of life. You may use all of your senses and there is a wealth of opportunities to savor. Music, babbling brooks, birds singing and chirping, ocean waves crashing against the shore, wind in the trees or the patter of raindrops are sounds that get us more in touch with nature. Scents include flowers, freshly mowed grass, sea spray, and rain. Visually we can enjoy the beauty of majestic mountains, sun shining through the clouds, alpine meadows, multicolored trees, a magnificent sunrise or a sunset vista. Our tactile senses appreciate feeling grass, sand or moist earth barefoot; the chill of morning fog or dew and the warmth of the sun. I am sure you can think of many others. Take the time to revel in the mysteries of nature.

You may create a positive spiral for your spirituality by appreciating things that are good, being open to personal growth and savoring the joys of nature. Try to experience more of whatever delights you. It will bring more wonderful things to you. Get this spiral going in a positive direction.

You will not be fulfilled until you discover your purpose and get onto your path. When you stray from your path, you will feel empty and scared. It is imperative that you get to know your soul in order to discover your purpose. Your life, itself, is directed at helping you to make this discovery, as revealed by Karen Garcia's story that follows:

The Channel of Life: A Story of Divine Redemption

As I lay silently staring into the darkness of my bedroom ceiling, focusing on how dark, quiet, and lonely this particular night seemed to be and wondering just how in the world I was going to go about stopping this perpetual cycle of pain and torment I was trapped in, I wondered, where was God?

"Why aren't you here?—Why haven't you answered my cries Father?" Only silence—nothing at all; nothing more than darkness and silence followed.

The hours drew on and on and as the warm stinging sensation of the salty water washed down the sides of my cheeks, I lay there in bed wondering, *Who will care for my babies? Who will love them like I do? Where will they go when I figure out how to stop this wheel of time and get off? I really really want to get off.*

Just as the tears began to choke at my heart, I reached over to the nightstand to grab a tissue and saw this little white moth beating himself up trying to get inside with me.

"Silly moth," I said. "There is no light in here. Why would you want to come in here with me? It's so dark."

And then the moth said, "But the light is in your heart—that is where the light is."

"What?" I said. "That wasn't the moth…"

29

I thought, *Oh, I've really lost it now....* and with that, the salty river of loss, anger, fear, hurt, and loneliness came forth...

Who was there? Am I crazy?! Where's that darned tissue? Instead, I felt the need to pick up a pencil and paper and write. *Just write, it's coming*, I thought. So I did. I didn't even have time to turn the light on!

"No, my beautiful child. You are loved."

"How come you are here?" I asked.

"Acknowledge me today. I was in turmoil yesterday, but today I am found. Seek advice, knowledge, power, strength through me. I have come to you for this moment, only to guide you and heal you within. Happiness, prosperity and love are yours to give and to receive. A better light is ahead, sadness behind you. As you walk down this road and up the hill through the tunnel, you will find my light. I have spoken—you must rest now. Goodbye, my child—I love you."

And with these words, I was redeemed. This was the very last night I spent in darkness. Through the veils of time and space, my Father reached forth and cleared away my tears, my loneliness and my sorrows. To this day, He and the many others He sends as His council cleanse my heart and fill me with the Divine Love and Light.

This was how I was introduced to channeling. This was back in 1991 when, as a single mother, I was just returning from up north caring for my beautiful grandmother who had just passed over into God's loving hands. I was trying to figure out how I was going to keep a roof over the heads of my two beautiful boys. All I had to do was ask. It was literally that easy. I know, easy for me to say. They say some of us have to literally be brought to our knees in order to hear God speak. When in actuality, if you quiet your mind, as in some form of prayer or meditation, you can learn to hear His voice anytime you wish. He is always with you and when you write down what you hear, this becomes a valuable record of your channeled messages of His Love.

This experience forever changed the lives of my two beautiful sons and me. I literally got up after receiving that first message and flushed the bottle of Vicodin down the toilet. You can feel the sincerity of His messages way deep in your heart. There is no mistaking them and, therefore, no need for fear.

I have come to learn that the innocent songs made up by me, that young little girl so long ago on her way to school, were the songs that were being sung with me by God and his angels. Have you ever wondered where this music comes from? God's precious light is that close to us. It's always there. You just need to trust your intuition, your thoughts and most of all your heart. As children, it comes very easily. But sometimes as adults we get filled with life and pain, and learn to block this light out. So, do yourself a favor and re-open the lines of communication. Free yourself and allow this Divine Love to fulfill every dream and happiness you have ever thought possible. It's all there—meditate, journal your thoughts, dreams, and even those times when you feel you are talking to yourself. Yes, we all have our little talks with God—even when you think He's not listening—He is and with oh so much love. Become aware of the voice within!

It was these messages that saved my life—That Gave My Life Back to Me!—that brought me through a time of loneliness and despair so dark that only a little moth with the light of God could find me. To this very day the channeled messages I receive are providing love and guidance not only to myself, but to many others around and within my life. But I always like to say to anyone who will listen—God's answers are already there within your own heart—all you have to do is quiet your mind just long enough to hear them. Sometimes all you need are pad and pencil as tools to help put you on a path to Divine Redemption and Love.

Dear Beautiful Child, He is Love.

Aho!

By Ladyhawksguide, 2004 (Aka: Karen Garcia)

Karen Garcia discovered her purpose in life through listening to the God of her heart. She now devotes herself to channeling messages of hope and healing to others.

As long as you are experiencing life
your soul is developing.

Your soul is as unique as your personal history, for this is what you use to interpret and understand your experiences.

The better you get to know your inner self, the more you will be able to love yourself and others. Work to keep your personality in harmony with your soul. Your soul is always changing and this is what lets you be all that you can be.

Competition is unhelpful. There are subtle or obvious differences between any two things, so they cannot be compared in terms of success. For example, I could focus on how many copies of *Time To Heal* have sold compared to the novels of other authors. There is no identical book. There is not one that is even similar. In addition, my efforts to promote my book are different from other authors. There would be no benefit to competing and comparing the sales to that of another book. Competition crushes spirituality.

What are you doing to develop your spirituality? This is the single most important step in discovering your authentic self and must not be neglected. It may be time to examine your spiritual beliefs.

Years ago, I saw a poster that read, *Experience is what you get when you didn't get what you wanted.* I now realize that experience is what you get when you did get what you wanted. The very same experiences that lead to emotional upset are the life lessons for which you contracted. These enable you to balance the energy of your soul.

Your life experiences may be difficult, but they will not be insurmountable. Seek support for yourself and meet these challenges with wisdom and calm. You will be alright.

Ask the universe for guidance, quiet your mind and listen patiently. You may find it helpful to still your mind by listening to nature sounds, music, or guided meditations to enable you to receive messages. What is the first thing that comes into your mind? This idea was likely channeled by one of your spirit guides, a loved one in spirit, or your higher self.

Answers may be shown to you at a later date. Be prepared to move at the pace of the universe.

Nurture your soul. There is a direct correlation between your soul and the physical health of your body. Repressed anger and resentment can lead to illness.

I used to have a recurring nightmare that I starved a parakeet until it was a tiny compact little bird. I always woke feeling devastated.

I eventually had a dream about releasing parakeets to the outdoors. I dreamed I was in a house with four parakeets. I opened the door and unintentionally let all four escape outdoors. When I went outside to try to get them back, two unknown and two known parakeets returned inside with me. Two of the ones that had escaped did not return and, for some reason, this was not an issue for me.

I later noticed that the dream about the returning parakeets occurred after I quit working as an administrative assistant and began devoting myself full-time to writing. I was starving my soul when I felt trapped in my clerical job. The release of the four parakeets followed by the return of two new and two familiar parakeets was representative of me feeding my soul following my decision to leave my clerical position. This permitted new ideas to come in and enabled me to re-commit myself to old ideas that were thriving.

Are you starving your soul?

Improve your living situation to nurture or feed your soul. Create a space that leads to peace and contentment. Bring nature into your home wherever possible. If you enjoy the sound of trickling water, build or buy a water fountain. Strategically place plants or flowers, either live or silk, where they will provide the best opportunity for appreciation. Hang nature scenes, listen to music or start a small garden, if this will give you pleasure.

Be selective about listening to, watching or reading news. The amount of violence reported can crush your spirit. Reduce the amount of violent language you use or hear. There are lots of examples of human kindness that deserve our attention. Let peace be your goal.

Fighting life lessons or worrying will not change how things will unfold. Focus instead on being all you can be; a child of the universe with love in your heart. Keep your intentions positive and have faith.

When an opportunity arises where you feel loving, express it. Sending out positive vibrations will return more to you, even if not at that same point in time. When you catch yourself thinking negative thoughts, reframe them as something positive. At times, I have had to remind myself that the homeless person begging on the street corner is fulfilling his contract with the universe and learning life lessons. It is not for me to judge.

Work to overcome negativity—this is the greatest challenge for us all, but it is so essential in our quest for contentment. More people than ever are consciously choosing to discover their authentic selves through love and light. Now is the time. If you have not joined yet, start now.

Two

Universal Energy and You

We have a great deal of influence on the energy around us. I have always enjoyed enticing birds to my birdfeeders, but I lived in one apartment complex for seven months before I was able to get any birds (with the exception of hummingbirds) to visit my birdfeeders.

One of my friends noticed there was an unpleasant energy force blowing through the complex between the bird-laden trees and my apartment building. She suggested I raise the energy surrounding the balcony to a higher vibration to attract birds.

Each morning, I used visualization to attach a grounding chord to the balcony, drained the energy, wrapped the balcony in a candy floss cocoon of pinks, yellows and blues, and asked the universe to raise the vibration of the energy. Not only did beautiful birds start to frequent my birdfeeders, but my plants began to thrive. The birds helped to keep the vibration high, so I no longer had to raise the vibration each morning. I noticed that on the mornings that I took the time to raise it even higher, new birds would come to my feeders. I enjoyed a wide variety of bird visitors, such as American and lesser goldfinches, orange-crowned warblers, red crossbills, pine siskins, purple finches, doves and bushtits.

There were often up to five goldfinches in the birdbath that hung in front of the window by my computer desk. As they flapped their wings and scooted around in the water, merrily chirping, they splashed my computer desk and sprinkled my eyeglasses. It made my heart sing and I preferred to watch them rather than continue working and miss the spectacle.

I would have been deprived of this pleasure had I not learned to influence energy. There is something magical about energy that vibrates at a high level and we are sensitive to this on a subconscious level. When I am doing a book signing, I bathe the table and books in gold energy to make it more appealing to customers.

You have this same influence on the energy around you and you may change the color of your aura with your thoughts and emotions. You may help your life energy become more attractive to others and to spirits. When you are positive, you not only raise your vibration, you also influence the color of your aura or energy field which influences others' response to you. If you are fearful or angry, this can also be sensed. We have all had the experience of walking into a room and noticing the tension in the air. Use an imaginary sticky rose to collect all of your fear pictures, put it outside your aura or energy field and blow it up with an imaginary firecracker. Replace them with thoughts of optimism and success.

When you have negative thoughts about a person, this is channeled to that person's higher self. They may not be aware of this on a conscious level, but it will influence their feelings toward you. What you send out is what comes back to you. Focus on sending out love and forgiveness and see how this influences your relationships.

Although difficult at times, it is important to be aware of the positive aspects of each of your experiences. When you perceive life events more positively, this helps to bring more positive experiences to you.

I experienced an unexpected opportunity that I believe arose due to my enthusiasm and raising my vibration. I often handed out flyers on sidewalks and in parking lots to promote my first book, *Time To Heal*. On one occasion, I met a woman who had also lived in Canada. As we chatted, I excitedly told her about *Time To Heal*. She became caught up in my enthusiasm and invited me to attend a Healing Through Music workshop scheduled for the National Association of Social Workers. After I arrived at the event, a woman suggested I bring in several copies of *Time To Heal* from my car. I sold eight copies. All of the people who bought books were counselors, some specializing in working with families of divorce. Considering that *Time To Heal* is a story about a woman who rebuilds her life after divorce and makes her life one she wants to live, I felt this opportunity was brought about through synchronicity.

Our auras surround our bodies and reach out approximately one and one-half feet. If your focus is the future, you may carry most of your aura out in front. If you tend to dwell on the past, most of your aura will be behind you. Being in the present helps you to be in the center of your aura, which is essential in order to receive accurate messages from your higher self, spirit guides and loved ones in spirit.

There are seven layers in the aura. The first layer is closest to the body and represents what you are doing physically, such as relocating or exercising. Emotions and love relationships are shown in the second layer. The focus of the third layer is power and how power is demonstrated. Communication with the body and communication with others are depicted in the fourth and fifth layers, respectively. The sixth layer demonstrates how you perceive the world in terms of whether your outlook on life is negative or positive. How you present yourself to others is shown in the seventh layer.

Healing professionals and intuitives have various beliefs about what the different colors of the aura represent. It is best to ask intuitively what the meaning is of the color for each person when you are doing a reading. An emotionally, spiritually and physically healthy, well-rounded individual has a wide spectrum of colors in his/her energy field. Some of the associated meanings are as follows:

Red: anger, love, passion, creativity, hate, empathy, strength, playfulness, earth energy, and Kundalini Energy.

Orange: cleansing, determined, confident, protective, curious, stubborn, childlike, playful, impending change and growth.

Yellow: power, strength, confidence, no-nonsense, warmth, nurturing, and competition.

Green: change, growth, healing, unconditional love, envy, exploring, and earth energy.

Blue: healing, nurturing, change, certainty, confidence, cooling after an angry phase, emotional, detached, isolated, and lonely.

Purple: humor, laughter, spiritual, creative, spontaneous, independent, feeling special, selfish, and ego issues.

Pink: nurturing, creative, gentle, kind, and bonding imbalance with mother.

White: purity, peace, comfort, protectiveness, and fear.

Brown: earth energy, old memories, conservative, contemplative, and judgmental.

Black: healing, spiritual, meditative, comfort with being alone, old stuck energy in the field, criticism, control and limitations over the vibrancy of that layer.

Gold: neutral, healing, Christ force, and spiritual.

Crystal: high vibration, healing and high spiritual influence.

Depending upon your wants and needs, you can use these colors to influence energy. You may wear clothing, burn candles or decorate your home or office to create the energy you want. This will affect others' response to you and will also influence how you feel internally. I wear blue when I am writing, as it raises my creativity and ability to express myself. I often wear rosy red when out in public because it portrays warmth and affection. Orange is the color I choose when it's time for decision-making, or when I want to create change.

You may also use colors to provide healing cocoons for yourself and others. Each morning, one of my spirit guides helps me to send healing cocoons to a list of people. The list has grown considerably, so I simply ask that healing cocoons be sent to the same people as the previous day rather than name each person individually. Occasionally, I add names. I ground and run energy. Then, I ask that each person be wrapped in a blue cocoon of healing energy. As I swirl the blue healing energy around them, I ask that any pain and discomfort they are experiencing be pushed down their bodies and sent to the core of the planet for recycling. I ask that the healing energy be sent to where it is needed most and that any excess energy be returned to the earth for recycling. I decorate their cocoons with rosy red ribbons for unconditional love. Once they are engulfed in unconditional love, I ask that it be absorbed into their minds, bodies and souls. I then paint on some mauve to help them feel calm and some green to add a touch of peace. Red dots are added for energy. I request that it be enough so they will not feel depressed and will have enough energy and motivation to get things done, but not so many that they become anxious. Then, I sprinkle them with purple stars to help them to connect with the love of the universe and be in touch with their own spirituality. I finish up by tossing on a couple of handfuls of gold stardust to enable them to have joy, happiness and opportunities.

I had several people on my list for a couple of months and then missed sending them healing cocoons for three days in a row. I sent out an email to a few of them to inquire about whether or not they had noticed a difference. One who has fibromyalgia reported that she experienced more physical pain on those three days. Another said she became depressed on the first day and spent the other two days in bed, crying all day. She thought that was just "too weird," as she had been feeling really good for almost two months.

Chakras are the energy centers in the body. There are seven major chakras and 21 minor chakras, many of which are located just in front of the spine. Chakras spin similar to CD's. The faster they spin, the higher the color, so the root spins slower than the crown chakra. The colors of the chakras correspond to the color spectrum vibration. They are as follows:

The first chakra or root at the base of the spine is your base of support. This chakra facilitates grounding, which means your connections to the Earth. Good grounding prevents you from falling and banging into things. Wearing red helps you to be grounded, which is required for accuracy when using your intuition.

Located just below the navel, the second chakra or sacral is related to desire and pleasure. It also facilitates decision-making and assertiveness. Wearing orange promotes change in your life.

The will to think, which results in power, originates in the third chakra or solar plexus just above the navel. This is also your emotional center and is represented by the color yellow. Wearing or being around yellow helps you to be more emotionally expressive.

The fourth chakra or heart is located between the nipples. The color is green and it is all about love, compassion and wisdom. Sometimes, the color is pink and this is representative of unconditional love.

The fifth chakra or throat represents the will to express yourself and communicate. Wear blue to enable you to speak the truth, to promote creativity and to encourage others to listen to you.

Located at the forehead, the sixth chakra or brow is the center for intuition, compassion and wisdom. The color is indigo or purplish-blue.

The seventh chakra or crown is related to higher will and knowing, and is situated at the top of the head. The color is violet or white. When you are disconnected from your higher power, this chakra is closed. We automatically receive cosmic energy through our crowns.

It is important that energy flows through each of your chakras. You may assist this process through grounding and running energy. I always ground and run energy before meditating.

Meditation provides better rest for the mind than sleep. It allows us to connect with the love of the universe. Meditation opens up our creative channels and contributes to our sense of peacefulness. It is an opportunity to absorb energy from the universe.

If you need a mental break, you can meditate by taking yourself to what one of my friends calls her "happy place." Simply imagine being somewhere that distracts you, such as beside a lake, next to the ocean, in the forest, beside a babbling brook or near a waterfall—anywhere that brings feelings of calm and peacefulness. Fill your mind with the sights, sounds and smells of your special place.

There are numerous courses and books available on topics such as yoga, tai chi, and meditation that provide ideas about how to become more centered in life. You may meditate simply by relaxing and focusing your mind. Many people are in a meditative state when involved in activities that require quiet and focus, such as walking, painting, making jewelry, running, etc.

I was fortunate to have been taught a grounding and cleansing ritual that greatly contributes to my creativity and peace of mind. I was surprised to discover that meditation can become addictive. At times, I am reluctant to slow down enough to meditate, but I never regret spending the time when I am successful. At other times, I can hardly wait to meditate because of the escape that it provides. I drift away from reality and afterwards feel refreshed and energized. My body is relaxed, my mind is calm and I feel ready to take on the rest of the day. If you meditate regularly enough, you will eventually reach the altered state of bliss and you will hardly be able to wait until the next time.

The following is a simple meditation which will help you get the day off to a good start, or calm you for a good night's sleep.

Take slow breaths in and out and imagine mother Earth's energy which is red, coming up to your ankles...your knees...your hips...all the way to your heart. Circle the red in a clockwise direction in your heart. Now bring cosmic white energy down through your crown to your heart. Mix the white in with the red in a clockwise direction, like a candy cane. Keep mixing it until it is pink unconditional love. It does not matter if you cannot see it, just pretend. Allow unconditional love to fill up your heart until you cannot hold it anymore and then allow love to seep to your arms and legs...then into your body, mind, and soul.

I used to do this meditation every day before writing. On one day in particular, I had been busily writing all morning and felt I needed a break. I sat on the couch to meditate, but I soon felt an overwhelming urge to go to my bed and lie down. I rarely napped midday, but I went anyway. I laid on my bed and almost immediately went into an altered state.

All of a sudden, I felt like somebody had taken the heel of a hand and shoved me in the nose. I bolted into a sitting position. I saw an image of a huge double-bordered yellow neon light surrounding shiny gold embossed block letters, *TIME TO HEAL*. I knew without a doubt that I was meant to change the title of the book I was writing from *A New Beginning* to *Time To Heal*. Since then, I have experienced many other revelations or answers through meditation, but even when I do not I appreciate the feeling of calm that envelopes me.

You may use the following meditation exercise when you simply want to relax and receive information from your higher self:

Bring yourself into a meditative state. Focus on your breathing. Inhale and exhale comfortably.

What is your first impression?

Where does this lead you?

Focus on being in the present.

Notice how it feels to simply sit.

Notice what comes to you.

Use your journal to write about this experience. Messages may come to you as you are writing. You may also write these in your journal.

The following is a more detailed and in-depth grounding and cleansing ritual that I use on at least a daily basis. If you have difficulty falling asleep, grounding and running energy while lying in bed will usually put you to sleep. It works well at bedtime and in the middle of the night. Grounding and running energy is also a great start for the day. It is best to be in a sitting position to reduce the likelihood that you will fall back to sleep.

Find a quiet, comfortable place. You may listen to instrumental music or nature sounds, but once you have more practice you may discover that you can meditate in almost any situation. Meditation is time you spend with yourself and the moment. It is a gift you give to yourself.

Grounding and Running Energy

I recommend you sit down when first learning this technique to help you to avoid nodding off. The most important thing is that you are comfortable. I used to do most of my phone readings sitting on my bed, leaning against pillows that were stacked against the wall. My feet were not even on the ground. I commonly run and ground energy lying on my side on my bed. I do not recommend this in the beginning unless you have some medical reason why you cannot sit with your feet on the floor. Most importantly—remember to breathe.

Release the grounding tube you have attached to the base of your spine. Let it fall all the way down to the core of the planet to be recycled.

Build yourself a new grounding tube. Make it the same size as the base of you and about one and one-half feet bigger all the way around. Attach it firmly to the base of your spine. Let it drop and unfold down thousands of miles all the way to the core of the planet. Attach it firmly to the core of the planet. Pull it taut. Release any energy that is not yours. Let it flow down your body, through the grounding tube and all the way to the core of the planet to be recycled.

Imagine that the soles of your feet are like camera lens. Open them and bring up some nice clean mother earth's energy. Bring this energy up to your feet…draw it up to your ankles…draw it up to your knees…draw it up to your hips…flush your hips. Send it down the grounding tube all the way to the core of the planet to be recycled.

Draw up more mother earth's energy, up to your feet…draw it up to your ankles…draw it up to your knees…draw it up to your hips…flush your hips. Send it down the grounding tube all the way to the core of the planet to be recycled. Leave this energy running.

Travel out to the edge of the universe and take some nice, clean cosmic energy. Add a tint of white to this energy. Bring this energy in through your crown at the top of your head. Let it run down the back of your head, across your shoulders, down the four channels of your back and to the base of your spine. Flush your hips with 10% of this energy and send it down the grounding tube all the way to the core of the planet to be recycled.

Reach down and grab a handful of mother earth's energy. Bring it up and blend it with the energy left at the base of your spine. When it is fully blended, use it to spin your first chakra at the base of your spine. Bring it up and spin your second chakra just below your navel. Bring it up and spin the third chakra just above your navel. Bring it up and spin the fourth chakra at your heart. Bring it up and spin the fifth chakra at your throat. Bring it up and spin the sixth chakra at your brow. Bring it up and spin the seventh chakra at your crown and let it fountain out your crown about one and one-half feet.

Travel out to the edge of the universe, again. Take some nice, clean cosmic energy. Add a tint of white to this energy. Bring this energy in through your crown at the top of your head. Let it run down the back of your head, across your shoulders, down the four channels of your back and to the base of your spine. Flush your hips with 10% of this energy and send it down the grounding tube all the way to the core of the planet to be recycled.

Reach down and grab a handful of mother earth's energy. Bring it up and blend it with the energy left at the base of your spine. When it is fully blended, use it to spin your first chakra. Bring it up and spin your second chakra. Bring it up and spin the third chakra. Bring it up and spin the fourth chakra. Bring it up and spin the fifth chakra. Take 1/3 of this energy and send it across both of your shoulders and down both arms to rinse out your creative channels. Let it rinse your fingers and hands and fountain out the palms about one and one-half feet. Take the two-third's energy left waiting at your throat and bring it up to spin the sixth chakra. Bring it up and spin the seventh chakra and let it fountain out the crown about one and one-half feet. Leave this energy running.

Imagine that you have a huge golden sun above your head. Call back all of your energy that is your own special vibration. Call back all of your energy that you have let others have and any energy you have left places. Call it all back to the golden sun over your head, until it is about ready to burst. Crack that sun open and dump this energy into your crown so that it runs down the back channels, up the front and showers all over your aura. Put up one more golden sun and call back any more of your energy that is left out there. Crack it open and dump it into your crown so that it runs down the back, up the front and showers all over your aura. Bend over and dump any excess energy so that your energies are balanced.

Because this grounding and energy ritual is lengthy, it is best if you are able to make a recording and play it while you clear your energy until you have it memorized. Or, if you have a friend or family member who wants to learn this ritual with you, you may take turns reading it to each other. Once you are able to run through the ritual from memory, it only takes two to three minutes.

Open your eyes. Take in some deep breaths and slowly let them out. If you wish to continue, you may keep your eyes closed. See what comes to you.

If you are experiencing difficulty stilling your mind, you may repeat the beginning grounding sequence over and over in your head, as it requires minimal thought and will distract you from your thoughts, without interfering with meditation. You may bring mother Earth's energy up to your feet, ankles, knees and hips. Flush the hips and send it down to the core of the planet to be recycled. Simply keep repeating this sequence.

It is normal that when you first learn to meditate, you may experience difficulty in stilling your mind. It is important to try to relax, but do not fight the ideas too stringently. Sometimes, these are issues that need to be worked through. If you feel dizzy when you first open your eyes after meditating, think about bringing mother Earth's energy up from beneath the ground, up to your feet and hips. This will help to ground you.

You may astral travel during meditation and may be able to observe yourself. At some level, you may be aware of what is going on around you, but it feels like you are not really present. Your body may become noticeably heavy and it feels almost as if you cannot move, even if you want to. Travel to the astral plane feels so pleasant that you may be reluctant to return to your body, but simply thinking about returning will bring you back. If you feel out of sorts after you return to your body, you may repeat the grounding and running energy ritual to align your chakras.

The following is a fantasy setting I often create for people when sharing healing energy. Take yourself for a walk through the forest and come out into a clearing in the sunshine in a beautiful alpine meadow. There are flowers of every color imaginable. As you walk along the path that meanders through the flowers, you stop to smell the ones that stand out for you. You eventually come to another clearing of short green grass beside a pool of water that has a beautiful waterfall. Lie on the grass beside the water. You can hear water from the waterfall thundering into the pool. The birds are singing. The leaves are gently rustling in the breeze and you can feel the warmth of the sun on your skin. The leaves are various colors—light green, dark green, and some yellow, with even an occasional orange leaf.

Whenever you are ready, walk over to the pond and dive in. The water is cool and refreshing. Even if you have never been comfortable in water, you are now. After a while, you swim underwater and notice an underwater tunnel. Take a breath of air, swim under the water and through the tunnel. You will come up in a pool inside a cave. The cave has sunlight streaming in through a rock opening above. It is beautiful and serene. A ledge surrounds the pool. There is a treasure chest on the ledge. Whenever you are ready, climb up on the ledge and walk over to the chest. There is a gift inside. Take the gift.

After a while, turn around to greet a guest who is standing behind you. He/she also has a gift for you. Take the gift.

It is time for you to leave. Dive back into the pool, swim through the tunnel and come up on the other side. Whenever you are ready, go lie on the grass and get warmed by the sun again.

Breathe in and out slowly a few times and then open your eyes. The more open you are to the power of suggestion, the more you will get from the fantasy. The gift in the trunk symbolizes what you value in your life and the gift received from the visitor usually represents what you value in a love relationship.

Meditating will help you to become more centered which assists you in decision-making, contributes to creativity and enables you to accomplish tasks. Drinking lots of water also helps you to be more grounded.

For those who are interested in self-healing or healing others, the following is another method of sharing healing energy. You may send energy to yourself or others by envisioning the following process, or you may physically carry it out.

Sharing Healing Energy

Healing energy is used to promote relaxation, reduce pain and stress, get rid of headaches and prevent them, and help people suffering from cancer, arthritis, gout, fibromyalgia, chronic fatigue, depression, anxiety, multiple sclerosis and many other diseases. It helps decrease high blood pressure and aids in healing wounds, infections, and fractures. It is useful during pregnancy and labor, as well as for helping patients before and after surgery. People who are undergoing grief or emotional distress find comfort from healing energy. Healing energy helps the receiver to release emotions. For example, there may be a steady flow of energy down the body and off of the feet, as the person releases emotions related to past abuse.

Years ago, Karen and I offered to teach a Bible Study group how to share healing energy. After a demonstration, Karen and I provided instruction, as each member of the group took turns being the receiver or the giver, with three people at each of three tables. I had never participated in a group healing activity before. I was impressed by the tremendous healing energy in the room with so many people participating.

Healing energy may facilitate the release of blocks, which may provide immediate and permanent pain relief. One of the women later reported that she had been experiencing back problems for a few months. Her back had apparently been so sore at the beginning of the meeting that she had almost decided to leave, but she was glad she stayed for her healing session because the pain had gone away. She described herself as having been skeptical about the benefits of healing energy, but months later the back pain had not returned.

Always ask the person's permission before sharing healing energy. If the person is unconscious, you may ask intuitively for permission to proceed. Set the intent silently or aloud by asking that all that occurs be for the highest good of all concerned. Try not to control the outcome or have expectations. Trust that the highest good will occur and remember to release any pain or emotion you notice coming into your body by requesting that the universe drain this energy and send it to the core of the planet to be recycled.

If possible, ask the receiver to assume a relaxed and comfortable position.

1. Check the receiver's energy with a pendulum or dangling chain. This may be done by holding the pendulum over the respective area of the body or by simply saying either aloud or to yourself, the name of the area of the body you wish to check. For the hips and below, the pendulum should spin in either a clockwise or counterclockwise direction to indicate good energy flow. For each of the areas above the hip, the pendulum should spin in a clockwise direction to indicate good energy flow. When the pendulum spins in a counterclockwise direction, this indicates that energy is leaking from that chakra. If the pendulum goes back and forth in a straight line, this indicates that energy is blocked in that particular chakra.

   • Check the right foot, ankle, knee, hip, then left foot, ankle, knee, hip, then root (base), sacral (below navel), solar plexus (above navel) heart, throat, brow and crown.

2. Clear the person's aura of any energy that is not his or hers. Spread your hands open and nearly join your thumbs. Start with your hands about a foot above the receiver's head, rake down to below the feet and shake it off. Make your motions smooth and gentle, as some people—particularly animals—are very sensitive to movement through their auras.

   • Rake down the right side of body in one long slow motion approximately ten times.

   • Rake down the left side of body in one long slow motion approximately ten times.

3. Pain drain.

50

- Put your left hand on the area that hurts and ask the receiver to send their pain to your left hand.

- Ask that the pain be sent up your left arm, across your chest and down your right hand. Hold your right arm and hand straight down for approximately five to 15 minutes, as if brake signaling on a bicycle.

4. Seal area and bring in healing energy.

   - Put your right hand on the same area where you were draining energy and hold your left hand open and upraised to receive energy.

   - Ask that the energy be accepted readily and easily, that it be sent to where it is needed most and that any excess energy be sent to the core of the planet to be recycled and reused. Ask that any healing guides or teaching guides who would like to assist join you. Express your appreciation of their doing so.

5. Ground the receiver, so he/she does not feel unbalanced. Do this by either putting a hand on each shoulder or massaging each foot and lower leg three times. Meanwhile think about bringing up mother Earth's energy through the feet, up to the knees, and up to the hips. Tell the receiver to slowly come back to the room and think feet, feet, feet. Suggest that the receiver rise slowly, as he/she may feel unbalanced. Recommend that he/she drink lots of water, as healing energy removes toxins and hydration will help to remove the toxins from the body. The receiver will process things for the next few days.

6. End the healing session by wringing your hands together. Remember to drink lots of water yourself, as sharing healing energy also removes toxins in your body.

Three

Intuition and Synchronicity

Synchronicity occurs on a day-to-day basis. Sometimes, it is as simple as a parking spot becoming available last minute, a cash register opening up at the supermarket or someone providing you with a piece of timely information. Other times, it is being in the right place at the right time, and encountering someone or something. Your spirit guides may create this to assist you in pursuing your dreams and getting onto your path.

Provided you are receptive, you are able to receive messages from loved ones in spirit, spirit guides and your higher self. If you want to connect with spirits you need to develop your sensitivity and heighten all of your senses, as they will endeavor to communicate through a variety of methods.

You may facilitate communication with spirits and angels by stilling your mind. Let them know you are available and wait quietly for their response. Be patient.

Sometimes, answers come over time without you knowing their origin.

When we are children, we are more easily able to listen to our intuition. Most of us learn to ignore this due to lack of acceptance by adults in our lives. You may have been raised by someone who did not respect your childlike qualities and you may have lost appreciation of these qualities. It is the child within us that encourages us to enjoy humor, play games, tease, have fun, use our imagination and express ourselves creatively. These qualities enable us to be more receptive to messages from spirits.

Your intuition, which brings inspirational and creative ideas to you, originates from your spirituality.

Robert Wertz's story reflects the connection between spirituality and creativity, as follows:

Divine by Design

I was introduced to labyrinths during an introspective period that began in 1995. During that time, I was living in an artists' collective and spiritual school of the Sufi tradition. Sufism is the mystical branch of the Muslim faith.

After a two-year tenure that included participation in numerous yoga retreats and recovery from a near death experience, I received clarity of my life purpose. That purpose is to lead a life of service based on the creation of artwork that inspires people to embrace their spirituality.

During this experience, I asked that God either accept me home or help me heal myself, as I could feel my life force being drained. At that moment, time seemed to suspend and I envisioned a way of living in which my work is my playtime and my sleep is my rest when I dream and receive inspiration for the work I do.

The creative process is divinely guided and reflects our inherent spirituality. I believe that if we accept that we are spiritual beings having human experiences, we can truly experience Heaven on Earth!

Since then, I have transformed divine inspiration into a photographic suite and various sculptures. I have also presented interactive seminars entitled, *Sacred Space Sacred Sound* and *Sacred Space Sacred Steps*.

One of the most divine works I have designed is the *Merkaba Mandala*. This is a labyrinthine mandala comprised of ancient symbolism inherent to many faiths including the Christian, Hindu, Islamic, Judaic and Tibetan religions. Rooted in Judaic mysticism, the *Merkaba* is viewed as a vehicle to attain transcendent states of awareness in order to gain God consciousness. The Mandala, an ancient Sanskrit word for circle (representing the universe), is viewed as an archetype for universal order. The *Merkaba Mandala* is a physical representation of the geometric-harmonic vision of this archetype and may be used to achieve an expanded state of conscious awareness.

Introduction to Labyrinths and Mandalas

Based in ancient tradition, the sacred labyrinth and mandala symbols are recognized as powerful healing tools that have received recent increased attention among the spiritual and medical professions. My introduction to these symbols occurred during participation in the recreation of a full scale Chartean labyrinth. The original labyrinth, located at the cathedral in Chartres, France, was created during the Middle Ages and used by Christian pilgrims as an alternative to undertaking the dangerous journey to the Holy Land.

The inspiration for the *Merkaba Mandala* resulted from personal observation of the unwillingness of certain people to walk the Chartean labyrinth. Upon inquiry, I determined that the majority of these people were of the Jewish faith and did not desire to embrace a Christian tradition.

One evening, I received divine inspiration in the form of the thought, *Wouldn't it be wonderful if there was a labyrinth based on the Star of David that would be available for people of the Jewish faith?* At that moment, I shifted into a trance-like state and channeled the exact form of the inner circuit or path that comprises the *Merkaba Mandala*.

The *Merkaba Mandala* is a physical manifestation of the Divine Order of the Universe as represented by the dynamic, yet symmetrical form. As such, the *Merkaba Mandala* is a symbolic invitation to embrace the principle that God is everywhere and that we are one with God.

In Closing

A young man once desired to become an architect—an architect that would build things and become great in the mind of men. God had another plan, which was to use this man to build things that would cause the minds of men to think greatly.

This young man was to become an Architect of Peace. He became the caretaker of a gift that would sow the seeds of peace among the minds of men—men who might normally respond to indiscretion by waging war.

The *Merkaba Mandala* is a gift—Created by God, through me, for you.

Robert G. Wertz
Divine by Design
www.robert-wertz-design.com
San Diego, California

In a good counseling session, it is the questions the counselor asks that facilitate change. People are usually able to use their intuition to find the answers most suitable for themselves when appropriate questions are asked.

You may quietly ask your own questions, but be patient in waiting for solutions. Let nature's source determine the pace at which your soul will evolve. It cannot be forced. You may facilitate this process by being open and receptive.

Create an environment of receptivity
so you may use your inner self to find the answers.

Keep your mind open and pay attention to what stands out. It will help you to follow your intuition. List your options. Which ones light up? Notice the energy around them. Which ones quicken your pulse, or make your heart beat a little faster?

Some people say that when it is meant to be everything falls into place. This may be true, but a path may also be paved with obstacles. A path may be smooth in places, but challenges are inevitable and, if you think they are not, you will give up when you encounter them. Expect them, revel in them and have fun overcoming them. They invite opportunities for creativity and building self-confidence.

When you attract occurrences, people and locales into your life, each one comes for a special reason. It may be for the purpose of encouraging you to change your route on the way to your dream. It may be a connection with somebody who will help you, or connect you with somebody else. Synchronicity may develop your spirituality and help you get onto your path. At other times, it may occur to provide a life lesson for you or someone else. Sometimes, synchronicity provides an internal experience through dreams, visions or déjà vu for the purpose of getting you ready for future events.

Synchronicity has a way of reuniting loved ones when least expected and intuition can also be a miraculous tool as evidenced by the following example:

Desert Miracles

I was placed in an orphanage when I was only two days old. One of the other boys and I became like brothers. We were inseparable. When I was eight years old, my grandparents came and adopted me. I never returned to the orphanage to visit my childhood companion. My grandfather, however, died three months later and my grandmother died when I was 14 years old, so I was forced to grow up quickly.

Twenty-seven years later, I accompanied a Lebanese surveyor on a work-related mission in Saudi Arabia and we were supposed to travel 32 kilometers into the desert. The road, however, forked and we couldn't decide whether we should drive right or left. I eventually spotted a Land Rover with my binoculars. The vehicle arrived and all of the men were wearing shamags, the traditional Middle-Eastern headdress, which reveals only their eyes. When I asked for directions, one of the fellows laughed. I thought he was making fun of my attempt to communicate, so I asked my Lebanese companion to make the request.

The fellow commented, "You did okay." He then greeted me by my name. He pulled off his shamag to reveal that he was my long lost brother from the orphanage. He had apparently been working on a pipeline and was on his way home.

I eventually became Superintendent of Concrete Production and was in the Middle East building an airfield. I developed a close friendship with a man I will call Ted. We worked 12 to14 hours each night and rarely saw each other at the work site. However, the main conveyor belt broke and we were given a couple of days off, while we waited for the replacement part to arrive. Ted, two other men and myself agreed to meet at 7:00 the following morning to make a trip to visit the Rock of Moses, a rock that apparently spouts water. I was excited about the prospect and rose at 6:00 a.m. to get ready. As I was making the 15-minute walk across the bare concourse to Ted's house, all of a sudden I felt like I had slammed into a brick wall. My body started vibrating and I felt terrible. I did not think it was wise for me to continue, so I returned home and went to bed. After I rose at 10:00 a.m., I went to the lounge for tea. I was soon confronted by the Project Manager. A 100-ton truck had collided with Ted's vehicle. The other two passengers had been seriously injured and Ted had passed on.

Ken Gregson
Dura-Shine Sealants Inc.
San Diego, CA

I appreciated the opportunity to reunite Ken with his grandparents and Ted. When I provided an intuitive reading, his grandfather identified himself as missing a limb and showed himself shoveling rocks. Ken shared that his grandfather had worked in a mine despite his missing arm. He immediately became tearful with the recognition that his grandfather was actually able to communicate from the other side.

The following is another example of an obstacle preventing an occurrence:

Creative Malfunction

Another Friday morning meeting for our team of salespeople and one of the men was speaking. I picked up that his mind was on something else. He was cooking up something that he shouldn't be doing. I knew he had a past history of drug involvement. I got a message that somebody was hassling him to get back into it.

He asked me to take him to pick up his car from the repair shop, as he needed to get to a meeting. The car was brought to him, but when he tried to re-start it to leave the engine wouldn't turn over. I put my hand on the hood of his car and intuitively picked up that the car wouldn't run because he was going to do something he shouldn't.

I told him, "Don't think I'm crazy, but I believe you're going to do something you shouldn't and the car won't let you go. I swear it will work fine for you tomorrow."

None of the mechanics could find anything wrong with the car. I kept telling him to believe me. We left and when he returned the next day, the car immediately started. He never told me the purpose of the meeting, but he had missed it.

Maxine Whitfield
San Diego, California

The following stories are examples of people who put out to the universe details of what they were looking for and synchronicity came into play. As illustrated in the following story, one man sent his vision out to the universe and it finally paid off:

Mysterious Appearance

Many years ago, when my husband was working in the communications business, he was asked to record a book, *The Master Key*. He recorded the book for audio listening and became very excited about the contents—the key to wealth, power, wisdom, and health.

It was a very old book and when he tried to purchase a copy, he couldn't find one anywhere. After many searches, we ended up in a very old used bookstore in the middle of Victoria, British Columbia. The upper floor of the store appeared to have been an apartment at one time and was separated into small rooms. There were rows upon rows of old books, which didn't appear to have been organized in any shape or fashion.

We leafed through the many dusty books and took turns in various rooms. I walked on a little ahead of my husband. He eventually wandered into a room without me. All of a sudden, I heard a cry of delight.

My husband soon appeared, holding up a book in his hand, "That was a great trick you played, leaving the book out in plain sight for me to find!"

He had apparently found it on the top of a little table, one that I had passed only seconds before when there was no book on it.

Carolyn Howard
Parksville, British Columbia

The following story is about a woman who knew what she wanted for a new home and set out to *Make It Happen!*

Glad Tidings

My husband died four years ago. Two months after his passing, I had emergency knee surgery with complications that required bed rest and round the clock care for several weeks. During this time, I became very aware that my income had been halved and more money had to be manifested. Unable to produce on my own, I chose to move down. After driving around the area, I decided on a particular complex in Encinitas. I enlisted the services of a realtor who specialized in that area and told her to put me on the waiting list.

Less than one month after I listed my house, my purchase realtor noticed they were hanging a *For Sale* sign on one of the condo units that I had chosen. On that very same day, while my condo was being inspected by a potential buyer, we went to see the unit.

I instantly knew I wanted the unit despite the fact that there was no fireplace, washer, dryer or central heat, which had been part of my criteria for a new home. At the exact same time as I was viewing the condo unit, the potential buyer of my condo decided to purchase my house.

The sale of my condo and the purchase of another were completed within a month. I was still recurperating, but that was not an issue.

After moving in, I was so pleased that my original criteria had not been met. My new home is situated on a golf course and I've discovered I really enjoy golfing. The swimming pool is only a grassy knoll away and I swim three times each week. I feel blessed due to synchronicity.

Jeannie Ike
Encinitas, CA

Karen was looking for frames for a couple of her smaller paintings. She and her husband attended a garage sale looking for furniture for their children when she spied a couple of small picture frames on a table.

Garage Sale Find

I bought two great gold metal frames with double mats at a garage sale for only $3 each. Wow! At first, I thought my paintings would be too small for the mats. I checked with my pendulum at the garage sale to see if I should buy them. I had already looked in stores for mats and the 5 x 7 mats were too small, but I didn't know how I could cut them to be bigger, as we're not very good at cutting mats.

The mats were exactly the size I needed for my paintings without having to trim them or anything. The outside mats are almost a forest green color with purple/burgundy mats on the inside. I put my spring flowers watercolor in one and my clipper ship in the other.

Karen Nelson
Qualicum Beach, British Columbia

As illustrated in the following story, sometimes spirits or deceased loved ones let us know of their presence by moving things. They are particularly adept at operating electrical items and may actually turn lights off or make lights flicker. They may even make the phone ring and when you answer, it seems nobody is there.

Night-time Visitor

When I was in my early thirties, I lived in Evansville, Indiana and bought a house at auction for $4,000. It didn't look very special except, that there was something about the side windows that really attracted me. They were 13 feet high and rounded at the top, made up of many small panes of old glass. It was apparently the original schoolhouse for the city back in the 1800's. I began restoring the home which involved replacing most of the windows that were broken in the front end of the house.

The house had a door in the kitchen that blocked off the front from the rear and also closed off the stairs to the basement. The basement was comprised of two red brick rooms, with lots of crawl space.

One night, even though I had shut and locked the door to the rear of the house, I was awakened by what sounded like someone walking in the back end of my house. Both of my cats sat up. Their ears were perked up, listening. I called a good friend of mine that lived a few blocks away and she came over with her gun. We didn't find anyone or any evidence of a break-in.

She told me not to be afraid because it might just be a spirit in the house. I didn't hear any more nighttime visitors, but I noticed that items were often moved around the house. I initially thought I was imagining things, but then I began to set things out deliberately to see if they would be moved. There wasn't anybody living with me, so I figured it had to be a spirit. This eventually stopped.

After I had lived in my house for several months, a lady who lived across the street came to my door. She was elderly and somewhat odd. I had often seen her come out of her house, stand there and then go back in. I was hesitant to open the door, but it turned out she was very nice. She said she had come over to tell me not to be frightened; that I was in the midst of a cauldron of spirits. She soon left without explaining, but I took her word for it because I had experienced many spirits in that neighborhood.

Sherry Christianson
San Diego, CA

Being on your path is energizing
Each new day brings hope, if you let it.

Let the universe decide what benefit you will derive from each of your experiences. This enables you to gain in ways you would not have considered. I participated at a bookstore's grand opening. Book signings are typically ineffective in selling books unless the author is well known. I told myself I would consider the time worthwhile, if I sold one book and in that way touched one soul. I was ecstatic at the end of the day because I had sold seven copies of *Time To Heal*.

Afterwards, someone pointed out that it probably cost me more to drive to the event than I had earned from book sales that day. This thought had not occurred to me. I was excited because I had reached seven people and was optimistic that this would encourage more people to read my book and benefit from the healing. This experience would have meant nothing to me had I been focusing on income.

Two of the women I met at the bookstore had a cherished long-term friendship that I felt fortunate to observe. It reminded me of the special relationship that develops between the main character and her neighbor in *Time to Heal*. Once again, this validated my decision to develop this memorable friendship in my book.

You may ask your guides for assistance regardless of whether or not you are able to directly receive answers to your questions. They will help things emerge. I had asked my guide, Angela, to bring in customers who would be interested in *Time To Heal* and healing energy. I thanked Angela, as I was extremely grateful for a special day.

The other author left 15 minutes before our set time of four o'clock p.m. I asked one of my guides whether I should also leave. No, I should stay until some time after four-thirty. It was during that 45-minute period that I met the women with the delightful friendship, gave an intuitive reading, agreed to teach sharing of healing energy to two women and sold four copies of *Time To Heal*.

The Events Manager later told me that she overheard one of the women telling the other that she really liked me and her friend commented that she really liked my energy. These rewards cannot be reduced to a dollar figure. I believe it was more than coincidence that these women came into the bookstore.

The following story reveals communication from beyond that was life changing:

Friendship with Death

I experienced excruciating pain with swelling and extreme exhaustion. The local country doctor diagnosed me with Systemic Lupus Erethematosis, a fatal disease with bed rest and pain medications, as the only treatment options. After several months, I emerged from my bed and put in a call to the hospital in NYC where my sister had trained for her RN and subsequently joined forces with the doctors in an EVAC unit during WWII. She and the doctors had become very close, so a call to one of them would be accepted. They admitted me and selected the best doctor on staff who made several new diagnoses, with treatments for each. Every one produced only more problems, so after 15 hospitalizations they removed all medications and took blood tests every hour. I finally produced the blood test for Lupus that caused great concern.

Particularly weak and in tremendous pain, I had a near death experience. With breath-taking speed, I rolled down an enormous, rubbery elastic, dryer-vent-like tunnel. It was similar to racing down a hill on a sled. There was a light with many people waiting at the end. I was drawn to a hand that reached in towards me. I was tempted to grab hold, but ...

"No, I want to have children!"

The next thing I knew, I was back in my hospital bed and there was a man standing at the foot of my bed. He mentioned a litany of symptoms that matched mine exactly. He told me he worked on grants for lupus and had also lost his wife to the disease.

My test results were the most severe he had ever seen. He experimented on me to find better diagnostic tests for Lupus and presented me as an example at symposiums. I was told I would live a maximum of six more months and was permitted to return home, provided my physician maintained weekly contact with him. Sixty mg. of Prednisone each day made the pain tolerable.

When it came time to pay the specialist, he refused payment. He said I had suffered enough and owed nothing.

I knew I was going to get better. Constant prayer became my salvation. My recovery was slow and difficult, but I later gave birth to two children. I am now 69 years old and I still struggle with Lupus, but I don't let it get me down. When you make friends with death, it makes life much easier.

Jeannie Ike
Encinitas, CA

I developed life-threatening allergies to cats and dogs following a motor vehicle accident that compromised my immune system. One of the synchronistic occurrences in my life was related to finding a successful treatment to cure these allergies.

Rob and I met a man in a landing field at a paragliding site in San Bernardino, California. He advised me that he had previously had a life-threatening allergy to cats, however, he had received NAET (Nambudripad's Allergy Elimination Treatment) from a acupuncturist in San Diego and was no longer allergic. I was under the mistaken impression that there would be no point in my becoming involved in treatment until after our hypoallergenic dog had passed on, so I wrote down the acupuncturist's name to enable me to pursue treatment once we no longer had a pet.

Months later, I met a woman in a laundromat in San Diego who also told me she had overcome a life-threatening allergy to cats with the assistance of the same acupuncturist.

One year later, we were visiting friends in Denver, Colorado. They had previously lived in San Diego and suggested I seek treatment from the same acupuncturist as suggested by the other two acquaintances. Shortly after our dog passed on, I looked for the acupuncturist in the telephone book. Her business was less than one block from where we were living at the time. She and one of her colleagues eventually helped me to overcome my allergy to cats and dogs. In addition to receiving treatment from them, I was shown a method of self-treatment that involved gradual desensitization. I also used a psychic method to enable me to overcome cell memory related to having been eaten alive by animals in two of my past lives.

Nobody else knows what you want to do with your life, so it will be up to you to make this discovery. You may make a decision and plan. It is important, though, that you avoid planning every detail. You need to have a clear idea of what you desire, but leave room for synchronicity.

When you are making choices, use your intuition. What grabs your attention, tugs at your consciousness or tweaks your interest?

As I was writing *Make It Happen*, I was often asked when I would be finished. I would answer, "I don't know. Whenever I've said all I want to say." I had no set date or number of pages. I wrote ideas, as they grabbed my attention.

A quick method for asking your intuition what to do is to toss a coin. It does not matter which comes up, heads or tails. What counts is how you feel about the results. This will quickly show you what you value.

Be careful not to fight your life's path. You cannot carve it out in stone. Rather, imagine life as a body of water. You need to move with the flow and ride the waves to the best of your ability.

Personal gifts and talents usually reveal our passions and dreams. They speak to us and entice us to develop them, provided we listen. What has your intuition been whispering to you?

We all have intuition, but some are more likely than others to pay attention. We have all done things our inner voice warned us to avoid, or not done things it urged us to do. Have you ever had the feeling you should take a jacket, sweater or umbrella with you, but ignored the feeling and wished you had listened? Now is the time to start paying closer attention to your intuitive thoughts and feelings because nobody knows you better than your higher self. When you trust your intuition and choose to follow through, you will find yourself doing more of what counts and less of what does not.

Exercise to Use Your Intuition for Decision-Making

The following exercise will improve your ability to use your intuition when decision-making:

You must be grounded in order to receive accurate messages. If you are standing, focus on feeling your feet on the floor. If you are sitting, focus on feeling yourself in the seat of your chair. You may use one of the methods in this book to ground yourself or whatever works best for you.

Think to yourself, *My name is...* and finish this sentence with whatever your name is. Close your eyes and notice how *yes* looks and feels.

Think to yourself, *My name is...* and finish this sentence with a name that is not yours. Close your eyes and notice how *no* looks and feels.

Slowly repeat these two sentences until you are able to notice a difference between *yes* and *no*.

For me, the energy around *yes* looks and feels open, whereas *no* looks and feels closed. Some people feel *yes* in one part of their bodies and *no* in another part. Some experience tingling or excitement when the answer is *yes*.

Notice what the difference is for you. The difference may be subtle in the beginning and become more obvious with practice.

If you are unable to notice a difference between *yes* and *no*, ground yourself and try, again.

Once you have noticed a difference between *yes* and *no*, you may use this exercise to use your intuition for decision-making.

Think of a decision you are trying to make.

Ensure that you are grounded and think to yourself, *It is a good idea for me to...* Finish this sentence with whatever decision you are trying to make. Is the answer *yes* or *no*? If

69

you are unsure, think to yourself, *My name is...* and finish this sentence with whatever your name is. Close your eyes and notice whether the answer you received is similar or different to the answer you received when you looked at your decision. If you remain uncertain about the answer, repeat the exercise.

We have incredible power to manifest things in our lives, now more than ever. The vibration of the universe is changing so that we are vibrating at a higher level. Not only is this making it easier for us to communicate with spirits and spirit guides, but it is also improving our ability to manifest what we want. All we have to do is have faith in the universe and ourselves.

A desire for abundance is normal human behavior. Abundance may represent wealth with respect to material possessions, but it also includes such things as loving relationships, beauty in your surroundings, or peace and contentment. This will help you to feel a sense of calm with the world. You are manifesting things, often without even realizing it. Every thought and feeling you experience influences what you manifest, as this energy is sent out into the universe to be manifested and returned to you.

Exercise to Determine What You Want

This exercise will help you to discover what you want. Even if the answers do not come to you immediately, they will be brought to you when the time is right.

Bring yourself into a meditative state.

Pull your spirit and energy into your body.

Imagine that you are surrounded by angels and fairies.

Their wings sparkle and shine, as they flit and dance around you.

You breathe in a breath of wonderful clear energy and let it out slowly.

Everything feels good at this very moment.

One of the fairies lands on your shoulder.

You feel blessed.

Look around you.

What do you want to stay the same in your life?

What do you want to be different in your life?

Your spirit guides and loved ones in spirit join you. You can feel the warmth of their presence. They let you know that they love you and they will help you to achieve your dreams.

What could you do differently to help make this happen?

What do you want them to help with?

Ask them whether they have any messages?

Bring yourself back to the room and ground yourself by bringing Mother Earth's energy up through your feet, ankles and hips. Flush the hips and send this energy down to the core of the earth to be recycled. You may open your eyes whenever you are ready.

Take some time to write about this experience in your journal.

What did you want to stay the same? What did you want to be different? What did this show you about what and whom you value in your life? Which spirit guides and loved ones in spirit joined you? What could you do differently to help make this happen? What do you want them to help with? What messages did you receive?

When I moved to L.A. I needed to find a hairdresser. One of the salons I drove by one day lit up for me, so I knew where

I was supposed to go. Shabbihmahhah, my master guide, let me know which time and day would work best so I would get the hairdresser that was best suited to my needs.

You may find it helpful to write down the details or characteristics of something you want. Consider what is most meaningful to you and pursue this with passion.

When you commit yourself to an idea, the energy of the universe will help to make it happen, provided it is in the best interests of all involved. If you are able to keep this in mind, it will help you to be more patient.

You may ask your spirit guides and loved ones in spirit for help in accomplishing something, you may ask for information, you may ask for money or you may ask for validation for a decision you are making.

If I want validation for a decision I am making, I ask them to bring me a sign to let me know whether or not something is a good idea. For example, I might ask them to bring a specific and unusual bird to my birdfeeder to let me know whether it is a good idea for me to do something.

Ask your Spirit Guides and Loved Ones in Spirit to Help you to Make to a Decision Exercise

Bring yourself into a meditative state.

Pull your spirit and energy into your body.

Ask your spirit guides and loved ones in spirit to come to you.

Ask them for help in making a decision. Either ask them what sign they could give you or tell them what sign you would like them to give you to let you know whether it is a good idea for you to do the thing you are asking about.

Make sure you are clear about what you want.

Thank them in advance for their love and support.

Bring yourself back to the room and ground yourself by bringing Mother Earth's energy up through your feet, ankles and hips. Flush your hips and send this energy down to the core of the planet to be recycled.

Write your request in your journal. Write down the sign you requested.

When I moved to L.A. I needed to find a hairdresser. One of the salons I drove by one day lit up for me, so I knew where I was supposed to go. Shabbihmahhah, my master guide, let me know which time and day would work best so I would get the hairdresser that was best suited to my needs.

You may ask your spirit guides and loved ones in spirit for help in accomplishing something, you may ask for information, you may ask for money or you may ask for validation for a decision you are making.

If I want validation for a decision I am making, I ask them to bring me a sign to let me know whether or not something is a good idea. For example, I might ask them to bring a specific and unusual bird to my birdfeeder to let me know whether it is a good idea for me to do something.

I previously used a pendulum to obtain intuitive answers from my higher self. Once I became more accomplished at using my intuition, I would only use the pendulum to validate answers I had already received intuitively. I was eventually able to trust my intuition and I ceased using the pendulum. As a matter of fact, one day one of my spirit guides came to me and told that I could no longer use a pendulum as the "channels are open." Pendulums no longer respond to my requests for answers, unless I am teaching about pendulums in a workshop.

You may use anything that will dangle and swing, such as a chain necklace, carpenter's chalk line or a pendulum purchased specifically for the purpose. First of all you need to find out what represents *yes* and *no*. Hold the pendulum out and say, "Show me *yes*." Mine swings in a clockwise direction to indicate *yes*, but notice what response you get from yours.

Hold the pendulum out and say, "Show me *no*." Mine swings in a counterclockwise direction.

If it just goes back and forth, this means an answer is unavailable. At times, I would suggest, "You want me to decide myself," and it would indicate *yes*.

You must have proper polarity, be hydrated and be grounded before asking for information. Otherwise, the responses will be inaccurate.

To test polarity, place one hand palm down on the top of your head, hold out the pendulum with your other hand and say, "Polarity." It should give a *yes* response to demonstrate positive polarity.

Flip your hand over, so that the back rests on the top of your head, hold out the pendulum with your other hand and say, "Polarity." This time, it should give a *no* response to indicate negative polarity.

Next, grab your hair with one hand and say, "I am hydrated." Your pendulum should give a positive response.

Finally, remove your hand from your head and say, "I am grounded." It is essential that you get a positive response.

If any of these responses do not match, you either need to ground yourself, drink a glass of water or correct your polarity. Use whatever method works best for you to ground yourself. You may correct your polarity by pressing three of your fingers under your nose, just above your upper lip for three minutes, while holding your other hand on the back of your neck. You may check your polarity, hydration and grounding and proceed with your question once the responses are correct.

To prevent confusion, it is best to keep the language simple, as if talking to a young child. Instead of asking open-ended questions, make statements that require *yes* or *no* answers. For example, start your requests by saying, "It is a good idea for me to..." Pendulums are inaccurate when determining the outcome of events in the future, unless one of your spirit guides is using the pendulum to communicate to you. I previously used a pendulum to determine whether to make a particular purchase or participate in a specific event.

You may also use your pendulum to bring in healing energy, break up congestion and release negative energy for yourself or others. For example, if you have a sore knee, hold the pendulum over your knee and set the intent, "Please bring in healing energy." The pendulum will swing in circles and cease swinging in circles once the process is complete.

Let your thoughts and dreams guide you whether they occur while you are awake or asleep. The universe gives you all you need, so that you will be on our path. Be clear about your life questions and notice what your intuition or dreams give you for direction. Pay close attention to your thoughts, their particular purpose and meaning. What stands out?

What questions are you asking? Are these the ones that will help you find yourself? What evidence do you have that you are receiving information intuitively? What are you doing to overcome negativity and develop your soul? What part does nature play in your life?

Communicate with the universe and be receptive to messages. Have faith in your ability to use the energy of the universe to facilitate healing for yourself and others.

Four

Re-evaluate Your Life: What Is Working? What Is Not?

The first step to getting your life on track involves examining your life and asking yourself what is working and what is not. Afterwards, you may tackle each area in whatever order fits best for you, but you need a solid understanding of what to fix before you proceed. "If it's not broken, don't fix it" applies here. Over time, though, you may discover that your definition of what needs to be fixed varies.

The five major areas to explore involve the following:

- Spiritual beliefs
- Career
- Relationships & support system
- Where you live
- Leisure time

In which of these areas do you feel something is missing? These are the areas in which you have work to do.

You may find it helpful to write down the five major areas and jot notes beside them in terms of what is working and what is not. Sometimes, a visual list provides more clarity. What do you think you need more of in each of these areas? What do you need less of? What would you like to stay the same? What do you want to change?

What you want may be vague in some areas, so write what you know.

If you keep living life the way you are now, where will you be five years from now? Is this where you want to be? If you do not want to be able to predict where you will be five years from now, is what you are doing going to permit this?

During the years that I was making the most change, I was unable to predict what I would be doing even two years away. I was constantly able to marvel at the events that were taking place. Maybe this is what you prefer for yourself, or maybe you would like more stability and constancy.

Imagine you meet someone who is a Quaker. Like the rest of the colony, he/she is dressed in matching black and white outfit, with a matching home and prescribed duties. It is up to you to liberate this person. What kind of clothes would you buy? What places, sights, smells, sounds and ambience would you like to help this person experience? What do you think would delight him/her? What opportunities to learn and create would you like to make available? What type of work would you be proud to demonstrate and share with him/her? With whom would you want to spend time? What ideas do you have about what might be personally meaningful to him/her? What would you say if he/she inquired about your spiritual beliefs?

Take time to think about the life you would like to offer him/her. Maybe even write your ideas in point form. After this exercise, think about where you got your ideas. Are these your own secret yearnings? If not, whom are you letting tell you what counts?

Adolescence is the developmental stage where the required tasks involve experimenting and committing self to values, in addition to discovering sexuality and self in relationships. During our early twenties, we focus on finding ourselves in relation to career and relationships. If you have typically done what was expected of you, you may have missed these important developmental tasks. It may be time to recapture your teens and early adulthood and, in the process, discover your authentic self. Maybe you have accomplished these tasks, but you are at a developmental stage where it is time for change.

List your priorities in life. What changes can you make to allow you to focus on these? What things do you chastise yourself about with woulda, shoulda, coulda thoughts? A job can become stale and you can be stagnate in a relationship. Only you can make old things new and pleasurable. If not, it is time to move on.

You do not have to wait to enjoy a personal sense of fulfillment. What could you do now?

Loss usually provokes an identity crisis where we wonder who we are and what is important in life. We either strive to recreate what we had before the loss or take time to consider our options.

This does not mean you have to experience a loss to initiate this process. Being aware of feelings of discomfort with your current situation may encourage you to consider possibilities.

We are more likely to make change when we have a balance between the push of discomfort, such as *I cannot stand living like this anymore* and the pull of hope, as in optimism that we can make it better.

Change is what helps us get to know ourselves and grow. It is inevitable. Although painful at times, change provides an opportunity to draw on our own personal resources, gather our support system and test our faith.

When my first marriage collapsed, I was devastated. But this event is what made way for my new life. I cannot imagine having developed my current life in the confines of that relationship.

Consider the changes you have experienced to date. What have been the benefits? What skills and personal strengths have you discovered? What joy have you experienced as a result?

Our grandparents typically developed their endurance and maybe our parents' generation also, but more and more people are recognizing the importance of self-discovery. You may decide to grab hold of whatever time you have left and go for it. If you have children and/or grandchildren, you have the opportunity to be a wonderful role model. You may also serve as an example for your friends and colleagues.

It is up to you to make it happen. It doesn't matter if you do not know how. Do what you know as you know it and the path will unfold—possibly in pieces, but it will unfold. Part of the process will involve getting rid of things you do not want in your life to make space for new ones. You need to take the first step and be ready to take next steps as you create opportunities or as they arise. As you accomplish tasks, you will obtain more information and you may alter your course accordingly.

Create Positive Spirals in Your Life

Fear pictures can interfere and hold you back. This energy blocks and repels positive people and things from entering into your life. We attract what we fear most. We also receive what we put out energy-wise.

Focusing on the positive brings more of what you want in life. Living a life of abundance means developing positive spirals in all of the areas of your life.

When you made up your list of things you would like to keep in your life, did you include the little things? I love to hear birds singing and chirping. The sound of trickling water calms me. Flowers that grow out of seemingly untended ground never cease to amaze me. Does it ever strike you as just plain miraculous that you can go to the airport and only hours later be on the other side of the country or the world? Even the change of seasons is mind-boggling.

Focusing on positives does not mean that bad things will not happen, but it means that you will open doors to let in your life's potential, increasing the occurrence of good things. You have to believe in yourself and what excites you. When you start to experience self-doubt, focus on what is going well and it will bring more of the same. When something moves in a downward direction, do something different to get it moving in the opposite direction.

Excitement and passion attract good things. Living in a sense of gratefulness helps to raise your vibration, which attracts more things for which to be grateful and creates another positive spiral.

You may be struggling to get ahead financially. Sometimes, it seems it never rains, but it pours financial setbacks. Can you see the light at the end of the tunnel? What do you have to do to get there? Imagine yourself being there. What are you doing? What does it feel like? It is essential to avoid underestimating the importance of believing in yourself and actually imagining yourself living the life you want to live. It starts another positive spiral and sends the vision out to the universe. The more details you can envision to make it real, the better, as this will engage your subconscious mind to make it happen.

In order to experience abundance you must look inside yourself. It might not bring you wealth or fame, which are the common societal measures for success. What it will bring you is joy and contentment in the knowledge that you are experiencing whatever is meaningful for you.

If you look for the positives in life—you will soar.

There is an abundance of books to help you achieve, with a variety of methods to get the life you want to live. Thinking positively brings positive things to you, or keeping your vibration up attracts things at a higher vibration, etc. It is important to reduce your tendency to experience fear. Imagine gathering fear pictures with a sticky rose, place the rose outside of your aura, drop in a firecracker and blow it up. Once you have become successful at experiencing less fear, you will discover that on the rare occasions when you are aware of fear it is because you are meant to receive meaningful messages that should be heeded.

Worry and obsessing about the future slows events from occurring. Here, again, if you find yourself worrying about when or how an event will occur, put those worry pictures in a sticky rose, place it outside your aura and blow it up.

One thing that is certain is that when you are thinking positively, you feel more excited, you vibrate at a higher level and your enthusiasm helps you to make things happen that you want. In other words, if you experience the higher vibration of joy, love and abundance, you will be met with more joy, love and abundance.

There are many schools of thought regarding whether changing the way you think changes your behavior versus changing your behavior changes the way you think. Why not use both methods? I was not convinced I could write an entire novel that would capture the reader's interest from start to finish. I was concerned about what to write as filler between events. I decided to write three chapters to determine whether I could develop fascinating characters and be creative enough to make the story flow. When my sister read it, she could hardly wait for the next installment. Her reaction combined with my feelings of pride and excitement when I read what I had written convinced me I could write an entire novel. This is an example of where my behavior changed my thinking.

The first time I was interviewed on television, I told myself I knew my material and could present well. These thoughts helped me to demonstrate confident behavior during the interview.

Being involved develops passion. You may not know what will create passion in your life until you try it. If you are unable to convince yourself you are capable, experiment with tasks that bring small success. Your behavior will gradually change the way you see yourself.

You can start positive spirals, ensure their maintenance, and leave them to blossom. Set things up to start moving in the direction you want to go, release it to the universe and get on with another aspect of your project or goal. When you plant a seed, you cannot keep digging it up to see if it will grow. Hold onto the confidence that things are unfolding as they should.

One day, Shabbihmahhah, my master guide, said to me, *Little one. We want you to live more like the Dalai Lama. He wakes each day with the confidence that the sun will rise each morning and set each evening and that all that happens in between is right with the universe.*

Visualize what you want and let the universe make it happen. You will start to notice synchronistic events taking place and they will feed on each other.

One of the most important positive spirals involves forgiveness. Ruminating about the past typically does not create change. What is critical is how your past is affecting you now and what you are doing about it. Resentment and anger interfere with positive spirals. Negative emotions eat you up from the inside and erode your personal power. It contributes to a negative spiral, which over time affects emotional, spiritual and physical health.

When you hang onto anger, fear and resentment, you let someone who has hurt you in the past continue to hurt you. Is this really the person you want to have control over you and your life? It may be time to get the spiral moving in a positive direction.

The following is a ritual that will help you to overcome anger and resentment:

Forgiveness Ritual

Sit alone and write onto individual index cards each of the things for which you feel anger and resentment toward a person or group. As you feel ready to forgive and let go of one item, burn the associated card in a fireplace, a tin foil plate in your kitchen sink or someplace else where you do not have to worry about starting a fire. Stay and watch while it burns and disintegrates. It is important to wait to burn a card until you are ready to release your feelings. Feel the anger and resentment leave your body and personal space as you let it go. As each card reduces to ash, think of the strengths you have developed as a result of this experience.

Turn the negative spiral into a positive one. It does not mean you have to forget, just forgive. You will feel as though a burden has been lifted. There is no time pressure to burn each of the cards. Do them as you feel ready. It may take days—it may take months.

This can also be a healing ritual for couples who are turning things around in their relationship. Each of you writes onto index cards things for which you would like to forgive your partner. You should each have the same number of cards, some of which are blank. The reason for the blank cards is that there may be times when one of you is ready to forgive something, but the other is not. A blank card may be burned instead. Do not share with each other what is on the card or whether or not it is blank. You can get together once or twice a week for this burning ritual or you may schedule less frequently, whatever you decide as a couple. Spend the time together as each of you burns a card. This makes the ritual more effective. Share this activity at a time when neither of you is rushed and you may spend peaceful time together afterwards.

You may also use this ritual to forgive yourself by burning cards containing events for which you have not yet forgiven yourself. Burning rituals may also be used to facilitate moving on in your life, as evidenced by the following story:

Unfinished Business

It almost felt like Steve and I were soul mates. I hadn't felt this connection with any man since my husband had passed on five years ago. We had similar philosophies of life, enjoyed similar activities and he had such a quiet energy. The sexual attraction between us was amazing!

One day, I knew Steve would be leaving town soon, so I asked him how he was feeling about the relationship. I was interested to hear any positive or negative affirmations about our relationship. Within minutes of making my request, Steve was clearly distressed. It was as if I had asked the big LOVE question. In fact, it was nothing of the sort. It was more that I wanted to know how he felt about the progression of the relationship. Did he want to see me when he arrived back in town?

Anyway, he stood up, kissed me good-bye, said he couldn't be here anymore and quickly left the house. I didn't hear anything from him for three days and then found a letter on my windshield stating that he wanted to end our relationship. All of this would have been fine, but I didn't have an avenue for responding to him. I felt his inability to be able to talk to me face-to-face spoke volumes—perhaps a lack of maturity and avoidance of real issues. Truly, this was a man who had some unresolved issues. However, I had already let my heart get involved and now it was up to me to detach.

I wanted to write him. I wanted to call. I wanted to see him! My thoughts and feelings tormented me. I couldn't figure out what had happened.

Linda reminded me that when we experience a loss, we tend to grieve our previous losses all over again. I went to visit my husband's gravesite and was shocked at the torrential downpour of tears. It was very cleansing and illuminating. Most of my grief originated with losing my husband, not Steve.

I felt vulnerable. It didn't help that I was already struggling to find out what I wanted in life and everything seemed up in the air. I fantasized about moving my children and myself to Nelson, a small folksy town in another province. I could teach yoga there and write a children's book like I had always hoped to do. I drove to Nelson and the weekend went okay, but Nelson didn't touch me. I was still searching.

I was curious about developing my intuition and empowering myself. *Make It Happen!* wasn't published yet and Linda suggested I read Rosemary Altea's *You Own The Power,* so I ordered it from a bookstore.

I felt like I was waffling and couldn't get the grounding I wanted surrounding the relationship with Steve. I needed closure. I really wanted to respond to his comments and contents in his letter, but there was no venue. I thought burning the letters was the only way to finish the intrusive thoughts related to having them around. Also, I knew the only way to get through a situation was to get rid of all obstacles, the letters being one of them. I still had a book of his that he had loaned me, one I felt he would want back, given a choice. I wanted to arrange for him to have it, as it served no purpose for me and it was also a negative reminder.

I asked myself, *What should I do with the letter that Steve had written and all the notes I had written? Burn or save?*

My higher self said, *burn*. My soft self said *save*. Believing that my higher self was right, I took the letters out to the backyard fire pit along with a white rose that was supposed to open up when I got to the right place to live, but was long past opening.

While I was tending the fire, the phone rang and I said to myself, *I'm not going to answer it, but it would be nice if somehow the message left is related to what I am doing.* As I watched the letters burn, I could feel a sense of calm come over me. I felt peaceful when the last bit of paper disintegrated. Now, there was nothing to look at or go back to, only movement forward.

I went back into the house. There was a message from the bookstore. *You Own The Power* had arrived. I had been in the store only the day before and had been told it would be another week.

I decided to return Steve's book to his place of work after hours and drop it off in their business mailbox. They could forward it to him, if he wasn't working there anymore. Steve typically worked one week in Calgary and then would return to a small town in British Columbia for alternating weeks. This was one of the weeks he wasn't supposed to work, but his van was there. He wasn't around, so I put it on his windshield and left. I had planned to visit a jazz bar, but I was no longer in the mood. I needed to take control and have closure, so I went back.

Steve was expressionless when he saw me—no raised eyebrows, no tilted head, no nodding. He seemed empty almost void. He looked at the moon, as if he was looking for a message. I approached calmly and slowly. When I asked him what had happened that night, he told me he had felt entrapment. When I asked him what he meant by that, he said he didn't know. I gave him what I thought a dictionary definition might be and asked him again. He then said the entrapment was attraction.

I didn't get much of a response from him. No, "I'm sorry for any grief I caused," or "Sorry it didn't work out." Nothing. Steve was clueless as to my feelings and oblivious to his own. He didn't seem in a hurry for me to leave, though.

We had started talking outside, but moved into the back of my van to keep warm. I held his hand and told him I would not abandon him and that if he ever needed anything to call. I think I said it on behalf of the universe, not just me personally. The more I was in his presence, the more I realized how emotionally devoid he was. I ended the conversation. He got out and I got out. I kept walking, said goodbye and drove off. Again, he stood looking at the moon.

He seemed like someone else, but deep inside I knew he was like that all along. I had just been caught up in the physical feeling. He really hadn't ever been that communicative. I felt good about getting a couple of things off my chest, but I realized that I would have been fine with or without the encounter.

In only one day, I got rid of the letters, his book and had a face-to-face encounter. It felt good standing in front of Steve, knowing that I had just burned the memories of the relationship—not because of vindication, but because of closure. I didn't tell him I had burned his letter. I wanted to, but I wasn't out to bring him down. Rather, I wanted to raise myself to my highest level of integrity. I wanted to move toward the Light. I'm grateful that the encounter did not bring me down. I think all the time I took processing and reviewing my own issues really helped me to stand my ground when I saw him.

JP
Calgary, Alberta

As you agree to commit yourself to a life on Earth in order to overcome negativity, you might as well do a good job. When you catch yourself thinking negative thoughts, turn it around. For example, if you find yourself thinking, *I'll never be able to make a living doing what I love.* Turn it around to, *I can do this. This will work and it will go well for me.*

Living a personally meaningful life is what counts. The fact that you are reading *Make It Happen!* now demonstrates that you are ready to do something meaningful. It is up to you to discover what that is and implement it. It may feel like an impossible mission, but are you prepared to settle for less?

This could be the time to start an incredible journey; a journey toward making your life one you want to live. You get to start the wheels in motion to get the spirals of your life moving in an upward direction. Look inside yourself for answers. Send your dreams and desires out to God and then be ready, willing and able to go with it.

Life does not have to be something that happens to you

You deserve to be happy. Determine what you want. Make a decision. Find out what steps you need to take and go for it.

Five

Take an Honest Look at Your Career

Is your work challenging and personally rewarding? If not, is there something you could do to improve your current job? It may be possible to request a shift in responsibilities or a transfer to another position. If you are happy with the tasks you do, but are displeased with the company you work for or the people around you, you might consider doing a similar job in another organization.

It is a scary idea, but it could be exciting, too. Sometimes, a change really is as good as a rest.

You may worry about jumping from the frying pan and into the fire, so it will be important to research the job. What is the rate of staff turnover? Is the receptionist friendly and eager to help? Do staff members encountered during the interview look enthusiastic? Is the management style amenable?

If you accept a new job and discover that it does not work for you, you do not have to stay. The Bureau of Labor Statistics recently reported that those from the baby boom period worked an average of 9.6 jobs from ages 18 to 36 years. Unlike generations before us, most of us will not remain in the same career for our lifetime. We will instead experiment with a variety of jobs and vocations.

You may change careers several times and you may work in areas that are seemingly unrelated. Most organizations would prefer you leave rather than stay and negatively influence morale at the workplace.

Volunteer work can sometimes help you to discover new career interests or prepare for a career change. More importantly, it could be one of the many purposeful things you do in your life.

Finding Myself

In the beginning, my desire to get a monkey was not altogether altruistic. When I signed on to be a foster parent for the Helping Hands program, I knew the monkey I raised would be trained to help a quadriplegic, but my modus operandi was for me. In the aftermath of my jaw surgeries and subsequent recuperation, I was feeling broken and had no earthly direction for industry—no sense of what I could do for work and no inkling of what I could do to satisfy myself or feel useful. I didn't feel particularly independent. I wasn't functioning as I had previously and I was trying to work my way back to wellness.

Being inside our own skins, we don't always know which needs aren't being met or even realize what's missing. At that time, I didn't know any of it and I was too close to my own person to figure it out. But when Ziggy came along, she was a baby. She needed me, and she didn't care what I looked like or what baggage I carried. My relationship with her was a clean slate. She gave me a chance to start a new adventure, so learning about her became a quest. I had something else to think about and I didn't have to ask myself over and over again, "Why me?" There's no denying it. Ziggy affected my life in a big way. She tacked her needs onto the bulletin board of my heart, just as I had tacked up the letter announcing her arrival. I happily and ignorantly integrated her into my life; we read together, walked together, and spent every waking minute together. She was, and is, still a child.

But if you're enamored with the idea of raising an exotic primate as a pet, ask yourself this question: *Do you really want to raise a child for 40 years?* Part of the fun of having foreign exchange students is they add new notes of culture into your family's database. They are fun and young and hip, and best of all—they stay only a short time and you don't have to pay for their college. With our own children, of course their stay is longer. They leave behind permanent memories and are more expensive, but they still leave at young adulthood, usually after 18 years—a dog, a short life span—a cat, independent and temporary—a monkey, a lifetime of care. If you have no network of support, no organization like Helping Hands to bail you out, then you are opening a fortune cookie with long and sometimes confusing consequences. Your fortune may well read: *Person who take primate must not have sulky kids or snarly spouses.*

We primates expend a lot of our energies on emotions. Monkeys have those, but often operate on instinct or doing whatever it is they want done at the time. They live for the moment, while humans get caught up in the jet stream of time and forget to have mindfulness. Since we're always moving ahead, we don't take time to study faces or analyze the nuance of every person around us. We act like someone in conversation who wants to speak, except in the interim of planning his contribution he doesn't take the time to listen to what's being said. My father was like that. He would add a comment when, unbeknownst to him, the topic had changed. Most of the time it didn't matter because he was our father and we dragged the conversation back to where it had diverged.

We human primates also whine about how time flies and get nostalgic over past memories, which are mostly just a distorted take at what we perceive was a kinder or better moment. Most of the time we're living on autopilot. Then, the time comes when we have to face down some catastrophe life throws at us, and time's passing becomes agonizingly still, large, and overwhelming. Ziggy's growth, together with the pain of recuperation from all the surgeries, taught me to enjoy the days when nothing much happened, when watching her face and deciphering her body language became a source of wonder.

Even though Ziggy's vocalizations to us were limited, such as "uh-huh" for agreement, "hoo-hoo" for isolation, lip-smacking for conversation, "Heh-Heh" for alert-danger, crying for bitching or taking something away, and screaming for being angry, we were still dying to have her tell us more. We were like anxious parents teetering on the cusp between encouraging a child who wants to say his first word to rounds of sheer hopelessness with wanting to understand.

I'd ask Zig, "Do you love me?"

"Uh-huh," she intoned.

"Do you want peanuts?" I'd ask.

"Uh-huh," she replied. (Sounds oddly similar.)

But the noise when I came home from a short absence and she greeted me was unmistakable—a composite of all the sounds Ziggy was capable of, only higher in tone, squealish and happy. It couldn't be mistaken for anything but joy.

Her moods, too, and the idea of her understanding us were subtle concepts, and one-half hour spent in front of her cage watching her entertain us was never enough. Sometimes, when I tried to explain a look or a particular habit she had to other people, I wasn't able to define it, but I knew what it meant when I saw it. For example, Ziggy's play face was a goofy look with a crooked smile that told us she wanted to roll up into a ball. Other times, she attacked her tail as if it had a life of its own, and then she acted as if she had no control over whether it brushed her fur backwards or came up behind her head to tickle her ears. Sometimes, that independent tail curled around in front of her and stroked her face, as if it was a strange appendage that just happened to be there looking for something to pet.

Friendly intent and approach with Ziggy was a complex gesture; a whole-body movement using a grin, mid-eye closure, a lowering of her eyebrows, head-shaking and vocalizing that sounded like a muffled "uh-huh-uh-huh-huh-huh." And whenever anyone important to her would leave the room or was out of sight, Ziggy would plaintively call "hoo-hoo-hoo." That particular sound could never be defined as anything other than what it was, a sad and plaintive bleating.

Over time, we became good at figuring out Ziggy's signals and were able to decode whether an encounter was antagonistic or playful depending upon her facial gestures, vocalizations, and the postures that accompanied them. Like learning semaphore, certain looks became predictable. For example, behavior accompanied by an open-mouth, bared-teeth threat was aimed at new stuffed animals, the underlings in her cage world. Whenever she was given a new dollie— what we called her stuffies—Ziggy would scratch out its eyes. We knew this was her way of removing confrontation. She even took to removing a certain amount of stuffing from their innards, picking them apart at the seams so that some of her favorites became a mere shell of their former selves. But she still carted them around afterward, one at a time, as empty carcasses.

For those of you who plan on raising children or animals and have no experience, you are fooling yourself if you picture smooth days of standard operating procedure in the future. Oh, I don't want to be the wet towel here, so be somewhat idealistic. But it would be better for you to approach caregiving by thinking edgier and going in with more realistic expectations. Plus, since the memory of owning something is ever so fleeting, remember to keep a journal about your experience and your feelings so when you think about doing it again, you can remind yourself about the day your infant spit up on your Armani suit, the time you felt frustrated changing a diaper at O'Hare or the weekend getaway that was called off unexpectedly because of a childhood illness at home. Balance your writing out, though. Remember, too, the afternoon your child gave you a rock and he thought it was the best gift in the world, the time he matched the socks by tying them in a knot, or a pumpkin carving that was made better for his suggestion that you add a mustache just like dad's.

In my newspaper column and also in my journal, I have stories about the shock of seeing my Dalmatian puke-up asphalt on the salmon-colored carpet, the time our cat mistook the bean bag chair for a litter box, and the night I sat up in angst because I thought Ziggy would die from licking Neosporin off a cut. On the other hand, I also have an entry reminding me how great it felt when our Norwegian elkhound, Shana, pushed open the bedroom door several steps ahead of her visiting master and jumped on the bed to greet me, and the time my sweet old Irish setter tried to nurse a litter of kittens. Getting a truer picture of caregiving with all the days, good and bad, helps us to appreciate both the quiet times and the frantic times with equal weight. That much I've learned. The uninspired, mindful day with those I love has become my balm for the rest.

Andrea Campbell
Hot Springs Village, Arkansas
http://www.examiner.com/home-and-living-9-in-national/andrea-campbell

Maybe it is time for you to start your own business. When I discovered writing, my life took off. I was scared, but I was also proud and excited about what I was doing. I worked full-time in a clerical position and wrote *Time To Heal* in my lunch breaks and weekends. It was so exciting— it only took me six months.

The following is an example of someone who is in the process of developing abundance through following her intuition and developing positive spirals by keeping her vibration high through enthusiasm. This creates a path for synchronicity and attracts positive things into our lives.

Lost and Found

For a couple of months, I had been searching for a building in which to start a Healing Touch Centre. One day, I was driving into Qualicum for a Naturopath appointment and I was supposed to drive straight, but for some reason I turned right.

When I realized my error, I thought, *Oh well, I'll just turn left at the next street and that will get me back to where I was going.* But, I didn't turn left at the next street. I drove two blocks until I came to a four-way stop and once again realized I had made a mistake. I was driving away from where I was supposed to go.

It was a beautiful day, so I decided to park the car and walk instead of driving around spaced out. I thought the walking would help to ground me. I parked the car and instead of walking to my Naturopath, I walked in the opposite direction. I ended up at a shopping complex called Chilham Village. There is a lovely courtyard there and I decided to sit down to try to figure out what was going on with me. After I sat down, I looked up and noticed a *For Rent* sign on the building in front of me. This is the space I ended up purchasing. We named it the Qualicum Wellness Centre.

I was concerned about approaching a bank for a mortgage, as it was doubtful a bank would lend me money. I had not been in the work force for 26 years, I had no clientele for my business and the purpose of the business is Healing Touch which is an alternative treatment a lot of people have not even heard of yet. I was fretting about this over the weekend, but on Sunday evening, the gentleman who owned the building called me on the telephone. He told me that if we could agree on a price for the space, he would carry the mortgage. We hadn't even met and had only talked on the phone once.

Talk about synchronicity! I am really excited about the prospect of helping others and can hardly wait to get this business started.

Shireen Zant
Qualicum Wellness Centre
Qualicum Beach, British Columbia

If you are able to do the same job day in and day out for most of your working career and remain satisfied, this is good. I can't and maybe you can't either without feeling miserable.

I thrive on learning and I need variety. More importantly, I need to do something that is a good personal fit for me and I am not sure this can be found on the first try. Even if you do find a job that fits well, what about the fact that we are constantly evolving? If this is true, how could a job that does not change be a good match forever?

Creativity has the connotation of miraculous talent. But essentially, all work involves creating something. What are you creating through work? Regardless of how humble your profession, you don't always know who you are touching in your life and how. Although they may not have expressed it to you, somebody appreciates or needs your skill.

If you were trying to convince someone that what you do is worthwhile, what would you say? If you do not believe this yourself, you need to move on.

Francis Curry wrote the following story as fiction, but it is a true story of an occurrence in his life:

Benzene Doesn't Burn

Wednesdays were always good days. On Wednesdays, the engineering department rarely had any new suggestions to offer that would change operating conditions and thereby cause new changes in the operation. This was the day the office force had to begin to work up all their paper work for Friday's reports.

Today was a particularly good day. Blue skies and sunshine bathed the world. Thomas Mahoney sat at the central desk in his control room. The operation ran smoothly. The majority of the time, most of this oil refinery ran smoothly. Many units ran into trouble a couple of times each year. Operation Six had never had any real trouble in all twenty-three years of operation. OP6 used a heavy solvent to treat lubricating oils. So long as the equipment was kept up and men did their jobs, there would never be any real trouble. The company kept up maintenance very well. OP6 made money every moment it ran. Motor oils, industrial lube oils and transformer oils came out the product end in great gushes of barrels of oil.

Tynesey Ronan sat in one corner reading a book, another cowboy story. Tynesey always read cowboy stories. Jackie M'Sweeny sat in the other corner working on a crossword puzzle. They were both good solid workers. They constantly watched their part of the control panel and never let anything get out of hand. As chief operator, Mahoney had the total responsibility of the men and the plant. Ronan held the position of first class and M'Sweeny was second class.

They each had responsibility for their particular part of the operation, but in the end it was Mahoney who would be held responsible for anything and everything. They had worked together for ten years. Now, they were a really smooth group. When one made a move, the others always knew what he was about.

Capitol Street ran along the front of the plant. Those who smoked were allowed to stand out on the street and smoke. Once inside the firewalls, not even a small spark could be allowed. Firewalls completely surrounded the plant. The designers hoped the walls would contain any fire which might break out. The burning material would be contained until the company fire department could arrive and begin to fight the fire.

Outside the control room, three large petrochemical heaters and a furnace roared with the flames of the huge gas fires. The largest of the heaters contained four very large gas burners. Flames from these burners surged up the heater for forty feet in a column four feet wide for each burner. Even though the heaters were lined with firebrick, the outside walls were hot to the touch.

On days like this, boredom would nearly put Mahoney to sleep. An alarm sounded. At first, boredom and near sleep prevented Mahoney from responding to the alarm. When it did register in his brain, every fiber in him came alive. Mahoney jumped to his feet and ran for the door. He stepped outside, but immediately stopped. The harsh smell of raw benzene in his nostrils told him before the burning on his face began that some plant had a very bad benzene leak.

"Where is the alarm coming from?" Mahoney asked Tynesey who had run out behind him.

"It's coming from OP5!"

Mahoney turned around and saw the drops like rain falling all over. Some of the drops were falling against the side of the heater. Immediately, the drops evaporated.

Mahoney turned to his two helpers. "Tynesey, you guys run down Cap street to the South. Run as far and fast as you can. You might get far enough away!"

Ronan and M'Sweeny turned to run. Ronan turned back. "What about you?"

"Someone has to stand by the control room until the end. There might be something that can be done to save the plant."

While Ronan and M'Sweeny ran away, Mahoney ran back into the control room and shut the door. There was no smell of benzene. However, he could look out and see it still puffing off the side of the heater. *What to do?* If he pulled out the fires, the rising heat would still suck the benzene into the heater and set it off. Benzene doesn't burn. Benzene explodes!

If he ran away and the explosion was not a very large one, he would miss the opportunity to save the plant. All of their jobs would be lost. Fear welled up inside of him. His stomach constricted into a tight ball. His hands began to shake. Sweat popped out all over his face and ran down into his mouth. *What to do?* Suddenly, there it was. The answer. The large stainless steel desk sat in the center of the control room. Mahoney ran and sat down behind the steel desk. From this vantage point, he could see the entire control panel and clock. The clock read exactly 1:00 P.M. The second hand clicked off the seconds. Mahoney could hear the little clicks, as though they were magnified. As the leak continued, the claxon horn blared on. The second hand continued to advance one click at a time.

Perhaps it would be alright. Maybe it wouldn't blow. If it did blow, all the glass windows would blast inward and throw shards of glass all over like a hailstorm. When it did blow, all the air would be burned out of the room. Maybe he could crawl the twelve feet to the door. There was a self-contained mask outside the door in a box on the wall. If he survived the blast and the burning, he might make it to the mask and be able to run away.

The second hand clicked on toward the bottom of the clock.

When the blast came, he knew the flying glass would pierce everything, including him. The tremendous heat would burn him to a crisp. There would be no chance to get to the mask. He couldn't live through this one.

Thomas Mahoney's hands stopped shaking. His heart stopped pounding in his ears. The knot in his stomach slowly relaxed. He knew he was going to die. It surprised him how calm he became after he had accepted certain death.

He sat and watched the seconds click off. He thought about the guards knocking on the door to tell Hannah he would never be coming home. Now, he could take time to think about the hunting trip last season. He had hurried to get off work, get home and pack, get into the car and finally tumble out at the camp. Deer hunting was so pleasant. He could just take a stand and hunker down against a tree and wait in the warm sunshine. Sunlight filtered down through the trees. He had enjoyed the peaceful hunt so much that he nearly fell asleep. He did awaken to see the tail end of a large buck disappear into some brush. It had walked right past him as he dreamed away the day. However, it was alright. His brother, Joe, shot the deer.

The clock still spoke to him in little clicks. Hannah had been thrilled at the diamond earrings he had bought her. She had immediately put the earrings in her ears and stood before the mirror to admire them. It was true. Little things made women happy.

The ground shook. *Here it comes!* Any second now the windows would come crashing in. The great ball of fire would engulf the room.

The crash did not occur. The fire did not come. Instead, the claxon alarm stopped. Shortly, the phone rang and Mahoney answered it.

"Mahoney, are you alright?"

"Sure, everything is fine here. The problem was at OP5. Didn't bother us at all."

After his shift ended, Mahoney drove home and parked in back of the house. He picked up the evening paper and walked into the kitchen.

"Hi, Tommy. I am glad you're alright. I heard the horn. Something went wrong down there today, didn't it?"

"Oh, those guys at OP5 again. You know how they like to play around."

"That's all?"

"That's it." Thomas poured himself a couple of fingers of whiskey and threw it down. Then, he started into the living room to read his paper.

"You are into the whiskey before supper and you tell me that's it? There was nothing to it?"

"Nothing at all."

Francis X. Curry
North Fort Myers, Florida
Author of *Just Stories*
www.buybooksontheweb.com

This experience convinced Francis of his worth as a person. It also demonstrated the meaningful nature of his employment position.

When you are looking at your options, examine what has worked best for you in the past. Consider a continuum of dichotomies. Which do you prefer, or do you like a balance between the two?

- people vs. solitude
- activity vs. peace and quiet
- open spaces vs. security and privacy of walls
- variety vs. continuity and predictability
- high visual impact vs. muted and calming
- outdoors vs. indoors
- travel vs. stationary
- various shifts vs. regular hours
- leadership vs. support role

List all of the jobs and activities you have done. Add what you did and did not like about each one. Are there any common threads?

If there is something you are absolutely passionate about, you may choose to adopt an entrepreneurial role. This may provide the opportunity to do what truly motivates you and give you an incredible sense of accomplishment.

Previous generations taught that suffering develops character and endurance is a sign of good character.

Being able to set limits and boundaries about what you are willing to endure is a sign of good character.

If you feel there is not enough of you to go around, there isn't. This is your soul telling you that you are spread too thin. It may be time to reduce your responsibilities by saying "no," or extending deadlines and scheduling some time for yourself.

When my first book, *Time To Heal*, came out, I sold 100 books the first five days and I was on a high. Within a few months, more than 15 bookstores in Canada and the U.S. had picked it up, *Time To Heal* received its first magazine review, I was interviewed on Global News Television in Canada and *Time To Heal* was chosen as one of 40 books from more than 2,000 titles to be featured in The Independent Book Printers Catalog. I spoke about the topic of *Make Your Life One You Want To Live* in a bookstore. We shared lively conversation and lots of laughter. People appeared interested in what I had to say. Things were on a roll and I felt the sky was the limit. My vibration level was definitely up and it was reflected by people's response to me. Of course, the positive response I was receiving was upping my vibration and there was a definite positive spiral happening.

But, I was still working full-time and I could not keep working, marketing and writing at that pace. I took a few weeks off to focus on promoting my book and writing, but was called back to work. I returned to the job because I was not yet earning a profit as a writer. The job salary was excellent and I knew the more money I earned, the more likely I would be able to take some time off in the near future. My husband at the time had just finished school and had started a new business. One of us had to earn a steady income.

My new work assignment became more demanding than ever. It started taking over. I quit writing and I was no longer actively marketing *Time To Heal*. The job was interfering with my dream. I had a desperate need to get back on my path of writing and public speaking.

I was concerned that I would be unable to get back on track, renew the excitement and in that way attract what I wanted. It became difficult to keep my vibration level up and I felt like part of my life was on a downward spiral. After three months, I chose to resume writing and marketing *Time to Heal* on a full-time basis. I had to trust that the universe would help us to maintain enough financial income to enable us both to continue to pursue our dreams and goals.

I was soon charged with enthusiasm and believed in myself again. I was almost immediately interviewed on television news in San Diego, followed by four book signings/public speaking events, three in the U.S. and one in Canada. *Time To Heal* received another magazine review. Once again, it felt like the sky was the limit.

It is acceptable to want money, but having it will not lead to satisfaction unless you earn it doing something meaningful to you. Writing is what fulfills me. Not everybody is in a position to live a simple enough lifestyle to do this and I am not even suggesting it. But, I would rather go without material things than spend my day doing tasks that do not feel like a worthwhile use of my time and energy. The end does not justify the means unless it is only a temporary solution. Living an unmeaningful life takes its toll on your emotions, health and relationships.

Abundance isn't necessarily material wealth. It is our experiences. If you are doing work that goes against your values, it doesn't matter how much money you earn, it will not feel good. If your work involves shoddy workmanship, dishonesty, or misleading and manipulating people, it will attack your self-esteem. It is important to feel proud of your vocation.

Honesty

One day coming home late from work, a woman stopped in at the butcher shop. She asked the butcher whether he had a big chicken.

He said, "You're lucky. There's one left."

When he took it out of the case, she asked, "How much does it weigh?"

"About two pounds."

"Have you got a bigger one?" she asked. "I need a bigger one."

He hesitated and then took it back into the cooler with him. He didn't have any others. It was the end of the day. So he came out with the same chicken and said, "Here you go. How about this one?"

"How much does this one weigh?"

"About three pounds."

She thought about it, counted her change and said, "Okay, I'll take them both."

We cannot take for granted the importance of honesty. Spirit will bring it right back at us.

Reverend Dr. Christian Sorenson
Spiritual Leader of Seaside Church's TV Broadcasts
Power of One on XUPN
Seaside Church of Religious Science
Encinitas, California
www.seasidechurch.org

It is difficult to walk away from a job that pays well. Being let go can be the end of a life sentence. A job is not meant to feel like prison and you do have the key to open the cell door.

When I worked as a counselor for Employee Assistance Programs, I discovered that in almost every instance where a client was laid off, it resulted in a great opportunity for him/her. Each person was forced to consider his options and, in effect, was given permission to do something different.

If you were laid off, what would you do? Scrambling to get a similar job might be safe and familiar, but what do you really want?

You can do it. Be willing to explore options. Read, explore the Internet, talk to people. If you are wondering what is entailed in a particular job or hobby, call somebody who does it. Most people love to talk about their passions. If they are not passionate about it, talk to somebody else.

It is important to be practical, but only to the extent of reality. In other words, you have to have the potential to do the job you choose, keeping in mind that given the right training and/or experience you are probably more capable than you think you are. If you faint at the sight of blood, for example, you might get used to it, but it may be a sign that a career as a paramedic is not an option for you.

We need a certain level of financial income to survive. I typically took the road of accepting the job I wanted rather than the one that paid better. It sure made things tough financially. I learned that habit from one of my clerical positions during my early twenties. I woke every morning looking for signs of illness, so I would have an excuse to stay home from work. I decided to accept a drop in salary, so I could work somewhere I would rather be and this became an ongoing pattern for me.

If you are looking at a change of career you may seek professional aptitude testing, or you may do your own aptitude testing. Go through the employment ads and cut out any that appeal to you, whether you are qualified or not. Include ones that look like they could only be a fantasy. Cut them out and organize them into categories. This will show you where your interests lie. Which ones do you wish you could do? Make yourself a wish list. Some of the ads that you pulled look appealing, but are not quite the right fit. What is it about the position that appeals to you? What is a turn off for you? Now that you know more about your likes and dislikes, you are in a better position to explore the possibilities.

I consider the homemaker role to be a worthwhile career, provided it is fulfilling for you. You are the one who counts. If you are feeling content and proud, you will be much more able to fulfill your roles as parent and partner. But, if this is your profession and you are not finding it satisfying, all of the same rules apply.

Education is a valuable asset when looking at a change in career. You may be able to do a good job without education, but you might not get the chance.

One of my previous employers shared the following story during a conference with principals, vice principals and administrators.

Just a Teacher

I had the good fortune to have an afternoon off to go golfing. I went as a single and was grouped with a threesome of men, all of whom obviously knew each other. They chatted about their jobs in insurance and the pros and cons of the various plans. Neither of the men spoke to me for the first three holes. One finally apologized and introduced himself. He asked what I did for a living.

I hesitated before replying. "Oh, I'm in life insurance." My comment was met with shocked responses, as I had not participated once during their discussion about life insurance options.

"What company?"

"Mutual life edu.com."

They looked puzzled and eventually one of them commented, "Oh, you're just a teacher."

Anonymous
Chula Vista, California

He explained to the group of attentive senior high school staff, as they listened to his story, "They are in the business of preparing for death. Educators are in the business of life insurance for youths."

There are many content and successful people with limited education, but for many education opens up possibilities.

Most career changes require new training. You may be able to receive training on a part-time basis, while employed at your current job. Sometimes, it makes more sense to bite the bullet and pursue full-time courses. Do not assume that you need to take on the biggest and best training. On-the-job experience can be very beneficial.

Years ago, my husband decided to get a Bachelor's Degree in Science, with a major in Computer Science. During the first year that he was out in the field working as a systems analyst, he discovered that many of his colleagues were making more money than he was although they had only completed a two-year diploma program. Sometimes less is more. During the extra years that he had been spending money on tuition, books and living expenses while getting his formal education, they were working, earning money, gaining experience, and moving up the pay scale. On the other hand, when it came time for his company to hire consultants, he was eligible because of his degree and work performance.

What training do you really need to accomplish what you want? Check with employers to see what they are looking for and check with employees to see what they recommend for education and training to do the job you want.

Nothing will raise your self-esteem or outlook on life more than the good feeling you get from doing something personally meaningful. You need a reason to get up in the morning—something bigger than a muffin. Everybody needs to have something in life to feel passionate about in areas that matter. When you are doing something that excites and motivates you, you will find you have almost boundless energy. It seems to feed off of itself.

When you work hard at something you feel passionate about, it feels better. It is no longer a tolerance test because it feels worthwhile.

Luck is not going to be what gives you a feeling of satisfaction. You must set things up.

Somebody once said, "You're so lucky. Everything just comes your way." I felt offended. I knew I had worked hard

110

to bring the events about. Nobody gets everything handed to him/her. It would undermine my confidence, if I believed only luck was required. If that were the case, only lucky people would succeed. These beliefs will keep you from succeeding in your goals because each and every one will take hard work and persistence. Maybe in the past, you have never viewed yourself as lucky. If you are working hard and keeping your vibration up, good things will come your way.

Some people want good fortune to fall into their laps. They do not recognize the value of the journey. It is the challenges encountered along the way that make the outcome meaningful and worthwhile.

We live in a time-oriented society and most of us tend to be impatient. We want things to happen immediately. Imagine that you could have everything you want right now. What then? For example, one day it occurred to me that, if public speaking was immediately comfortable to me, I would miss the process and I would have to come up with a new growth challenge. If my books immediately became best sellers, how would I have spent the many months that were otherwise devoted to strengthening my skills and experimenting with new methods of promoting my books and myself? What about all of the wonderful people I have met? If our goals were immediately fulfilled, we would have to be incredibly creative in dreaming up new ideas to keep ourselves challenged. We are better off learning to savor the journey more.

Being passionate about your goals motivates you to take risks you might not otherwise. It encourages you to do more than the bare minimum. If you do not care about what you are doing, why would anybody else? To enlist the support of others, it has to be evident that you believe what you are doing is of value.

Years ago, my husband and I decided to lease our home and move full-time into a fifth-wheel recreational vehicle. We wanted to take some time to enjoy life, while we were still able. We talked about what we wanted to do with our lives and where we wanted to live. By simplifying our lives and greatly reducing our living expenses, we discovered our needs were few. This freed us to get out of our career jobs in which we both felt trapped. We discovered that old is a state of mind. Our parents were unimpressed and embarrassed by our decision.

It is important to believe in yourself and what you are doing. When you have doubts, remind yourself of the reasons. Change can be frightening, but exciting. Realistic challenges in jobs or hobbies lead to feelings of satisfaction. Maybe you did not perfectly meet the challenge, but you may feel proud about an aspect of how you handled it, or the fact that you coped better than previously. Perhaps you experienced less fear than usual. Maybe you are simply proud that you tried something new. Your occupation needs to nurture your soul. Use your intuition to tell you what would be personally meaningful.

Six

Sort Through Your Relationships and Support System

A Special Friend

I felt she loved me the minute she saw me and we became friends from then on. I was like the daughter she never had. We spent hours together and talked about angels, spirituality, letting go and giving it to God. My favorite stories she told were about how lovely La Jolla was in 1944 when it was a village and Gregory Peck walked the streets.

Life is such an irony. It was like watching a wounded bird trying to catch her breath on her deathbed rather than an intelligent spunky lady who did not lose her grace until the very end. She had suffered from polio as a child and later endured two destructive marriages. I learned so much from listening to her advice. It will be very strange not having her to talk to on a daily basis.

She was diagnosed with lung cancer six weeks ago. Her passing was swift and mighty with a force that was devastating. When I saw her for the last time, she asked me to hold her hand, pray and give her the strength to pass over. My intuition told me she had two days to live. She passed away 42 hours later.

No one else was as available to give me advice when I needed it. She was on exactly the same level as I was when it came to talking about psychic phenomenon. So many small gifts and little things will be remembered, but the thing I will remember the most is the wisdom in her dark eyes that looked upon me with admiration and love.

Does anything mean as much in life as a good friend? Love is all we really have, as we travel through life acquiring things and trying to show how successful we are. I am fortunate because I have expressed exactly how I feel with each person who has passed away in my life. It is important for all of us to pick up the phone and tell everyone we love how we feel.

Grayce Burkitt
Author of *Sacred Synchronicity*
San Diego, CA

Good friendships are invaluable. There may be some people in your life who are able to evolve with you as you pursue change, but others will no longer be a good match. You may discover you no longer have mutual interests. It is understandable, if you let these relationships drift away. Due to increased mobility, support systems are more difficult to maintain than they were previously. It is impossible for you to stay connected with everybody you meet throughout your lifetime. Determine which relationships are the most important to you and devote some effort to maintaining them.

You may sort everybody including friends, family and co-workers into two categories:

- Inspiriters (Those who you feel better about yourself after spending time with them.)

- Despiriters (Those who you feel worse about yourself after spending time with them.)

Despiriters

As follows, there are several types of despiriters:

Competitors

It is annoying to be around somebody who, no matter what your experience, can one-up it. Even with catastrophes, this can be irritating. You came down with pneumonia, but they had pneumonia and bronchitis simultaneously and it lasted twice as long. You had a horrible vacation. They had the worst vacation ever. On occasion, a person sharing a worse experience can help you feel better about yours, but on a constant basis from the same person it is invalidating.

Minimizers

These people repeatedly minimize your experiences. They use pat phrases that often start with "Oh, well." Such as, "Oh, well, it wasn't that bad;" "Oh well, it will all come out in the wash." "Oh well, all's well that ends well." The message you hear is that you are too sensitive, or you get upset over nothing. You try to justify yourself and before you know it a mountain has been made out of a molehill and you end up behaving exactly the way in which they accused you in the first place.

Mountains Out of Molehills

Julie told one of her co-workers, Shirley, that her husband's habit of leaving his socks and underwear on the bedroom carpet was getting on her nerves. Shirley's response was that it only takes a few minutes to pick them up and throw them in the hamper. Julie told her that it didn't happen only occasionally, but every day and it had been going on for years. She explained that it didn't make sense to her that he couldn't put them in the hamper himself. Shirley commented that they were only small items. To justify herself, Julie reported that he also draped his shirt and pants over a chair almost every night instead of hanging them up in the closet. This behavior didn't even bother her because he often put those clothes back on the following day provided they were still presentable. Julie ended up feeling bad that she was painting such a negative picture of her husband in her effort to get Shirley to understand her point of view.

Some people do not feel comfortable with emotion—yours, anybody else's, or even their own. After a while, you can recognize the pattern and realize that sharing your feelings with this person will not be a positive experience. If you tend to be an open individual you might want to minimize the amount of time you spend with these people.

Advice Givers

Many people don't like to receive advice. Even though some ask for advice, they don't really want any. Given enough time, people can usually come up with their own solutions. There are exceptions to this, but it is often insulting to have someone offer advice. If another person is quickly able to provide an easy solution, unless he/she is a specialist in the area there is probably something unsuitable with the suggestion, or you would have come up with it yourself.

Users

In these relationships, you are the one who is constantly giving and they are the takers. For example, you usually drive. You make the calls. You provide or pay for the food or beverage. And conversation tends to revolve around their lives. You sacrifice your needs to theirs and wonder why you feel empty in their presence.

Guilt Trippers

Who wants to spend time with someone who starts out the conversation by complaining about how delinquent you have been in making contact? You have not called recently, visited soon enough or jumped through enough hoops. These are the people with whom you dread talking and the longer you put it off, the more you are going to pay when you finally do make contact. They test limits in the friendship and use guilt to get their way.

Some of us have family members who are manipulative. Every year, the whole family goes to Aunt Bertha's for Thanksgiving Dinner. You do not want to go. Maybe you have children or a partner who also do not want to attend. It is usually a negative experience, but it is expected of you. What is the worst thing that could happen, if you let family members know that you will be attending other family functions, but you would like to develop a new ritual for Thanksgiving? Perhaps you would like to include only your immediate family or special friends. Maybe you would like to spend a special day alone.

Abusers

Abusers are critical and arrogant. They pick you apart simply because they can. You may find yourself quietly letting the person mow you down, while you sit shell-shocked.

It's time to either get rid of, or significantly reduce time spent with the despiriters. If you feel unable to change or end a relationship, only spend time with him/her when you are strong enough to handle the feelings it provokes.

Consider writing each of them a letter, but do not send it. It will help you become clear on what you can and cannot

117

tolerate in the relationship. It might even become the foundation for a conversation you share with this individual at a time when you are feeling calm and relaxed.

There is no point in responding with anger to the people you encounter who are there to help you learn your life lessons. This does not mean you have to lie down and let them walk all over you. Your role is to develop greater understanding and love. You may set boundaries and limits as needed in your relationships with others, but do it with compassion and love. Anger does not effectively change another person's behavior. It takes respect and love to engage a person's cooperation and work toward acceptable compromises.

Setting Personal Boundaries and Limits

If you are going to discuss change in a relationship you hope to continue, you must start out by letting the other person know that you value them and the relationship you share. People are generally unwilling to invest in a relationship, if they are convinced the other person is about to write them off. It is important that you assume responsibility for your own behavior and not put all of the blame on the other person. Whenever possible, avoid letting things build and nip things in the bud before the situation mushrooms. Sometimes despiriters can be turned into inspiriters by sharing your needs with them.

We all have obligations. Some are truly our responsibility. Others are ones we take on due to guilt. In these cases, you would be better off to say, "No." No excuses are necessary. If you are clear on what you can and cannot do, people will be less likely to pressure you. Otherwise, you may end up feeling anger toward that person for manipulating you, but will inevitably end up feeling angry toward yourself for not taking a stand.

Perhaps you have already agreed to a commitment. You know it is draining you because of the dread you feel whenever you think about it. It is acceptable to change your mind. At times, we become more aware of our priorities as the date approaches, or after we have already started a project to which we committed ourselves. Nobody is indispensable. Be true to yourself and draw the line.

There is a thin line between being assertive and being aggressive. If you are setting out to develop your assertiveness skills, there will be times when you will step over this line. It takes practice to be able to speak up soon enough to avoid letting resentment grow to the point where you can no longer appropriately express yourself.

The Fork

As I look back on my carefree childhood, I wonder when I first realized that I would have to be the one in charge of how I would develop as an individual. My older sister was a social butterfly. As a youngster, I was content to follow her around and let her do the talking for both of us. She did it so well. I preferred staying unnoticed in the background. But the day came when a girl couldn't be expected to be the mouthpiece for her shy little sister. This was the day.

The four children and their baby brother were like a circus of excited motion. They were going OUT to dinner tonight! Mother and Daddy were often invited to spend an evening with couples in the congregation they served in the small farming town of Melrose, New Mexico. But with five young children, extending an invitation to the whole family was a bit overwhelming to a would-be host and hostess. Tonight, however, a family friend I will call Mrs. Friskie seemed sure she could handle the whole brood and dinner would be served at 5:30 sharp.

The children gleefully splashed water on hands and faces, as they cleaned up. "Mommy, can I wear my Davy

Crockett hat?" Donald called, as he ran down the hall to the bedroom.

"No, honey. You kids all need to get into your Sunday clothes. Sally, can you help Howdy?" Sally was seven years old and her mother's little helper. She finished buttoning up her pretty pink dress with the puffy sleeves and flouncy skirt. Then, picking up her shoes and socks, she practiced a little twirl before heading for the boys' room. Yes, her skirt flared out satisfactorily— just like a ballerina.

Finally, everyone was dressed; shoes buckled and tied, shirts tucked in, buttons even with buttonholes, hair combed and shining, and the baby freshly diapered. Sally brought her young charge into the living room and the two of them sat down with their parents.

"Come on, kids," hollered Daddy. "We've got a few things to talk about before we go." Donald and Carol dashed through the door and raced to see who would get to the couch first. "Hold it," Daddy chided. "There will be no running in the house, especially when we get to Mrs. Friskie's. You'll knock her down!"

"Now, kids," Mother started. "Let's talk about manners. Everyone says you're always so well behaved and we're proud of you for that. But sometimes we forget what we should do at the table. What do you say when someone puts something on your plate?"

"Thank you!" chorused the children.

"And what do you say if it's something you think you don't like?"

"Thank you!" replied three of them. Donald made a rude gagging sound that was ignored by his parents. The other children giggled and then waited expectantly for the next question.

"Why don't you wipe your mouth with your sleeve?"

"Because a sleeve isn't a napkin."

"Why don't you poke your sister or brother?"

"Because they're not a punching bag."

"Why don't you blow bubbles in your milk?"

"Because we're not fishies."

"And why don't you hold your fork like this?" Mother held up a clenched fist.

"Because a fork isn't a shovel."

"Good. I think we're ready to go." Mother picked up the baby, while Daddy shooed the children ahead of him and out the door.

The family trooped down the street, Sunday shoes clattering sharply on the sun-warmed sidewalk. As they crossed the street, Sally carefully held on to Howdy's hand. His moist little fingers clutched tightly, as she pulled him up on the curb and guided him around the corner. The drought-stricken yards had long ago given up to sticker-weeds and horned toads. Here and there a straggly tree cast hot, fitful shadows over the walkers. No matter, childish anticipation burned as passionately as the day.

"Almost there," Sally sang. "It's Howdy-Doody time. It's goody-foody time. It's Mrs. Friskie time. It's almost dinner time!"

How exciting to be going to dinner. This was a new experience for all of the children. They'd had holiday dinners with relatives before, but never all of them at one time with someone from the church who invited them just because she wanted to. Bless Mrs. Friskie!

The seven filed up to the front porch, the children hop-skip-and jumping up the steps, and they were there. Mrs. Friskie opened the door and ushered them into her wonderful old house. It was dark inside, and almost cool. Heavy draperies blocked out the summer sun. Slippery horsehair chairs sat arm-to-arm across the room from a velvety purple sofa, plump with pillows. Enchanting, breakable figurines graced the end tables and sat primly on their own lacy doilies. Lamps with silk tassels cast a soft glow in the corners and caught the emerald glints in the eyes of a large tabby backing away from the suddenly silent children.

"Come this way," Mrs. Friskie invited. "The dining room is right through that door."

With a minimum of elbowing and whispered exchanges, Sally and her family found their places. Mrs. Friskie lit the candles and began to bring in dinner. Sally's eyes grew large, as the bowls and platters were placed on the table. Spaghetti with real meatballs instead of meat sauce. And it looked like the noodles were still their original length, not broken into pieces before they were even cooked. The beautiful store-bought bread had been carefully split, buttered, and toasted to a golden brown in the oven. A cut glass bowl held the salad; a work of art with its layers of lettuce, tomatoes, and fixin's not yet tossed. The dressing was in its own little crystal bowl, complete with miniature ladle. Perhaps the best treat of all was the amber colored iced tea in tall frosty glasses, clinking with hard, clear ice cubes, and a long silver spoon to stir in the sugar close at hand. No milk tonight. It was dinner out. Oh, a feast to be sure!

There was silence, while everyone around the table took hands and blessed the food. Napkins were carefully laid across knees or tucked under chins, and the meal began.

But what was this? Sally sat with downcast eyes, twisting her hands in her lap. She tried to get Carol's attention by kicking at her under the table, but her sister was out of reach. She glanced at her mother who was busy cutting the baby's meatball into bite-sized pieces. Her father and Mrs. Friskie were having a spirited conversation, and Howdy and Donald gleefully experimented with twirling spaghetti on their forks. Sally sat silently.

Mrs. Friskie suddenly noticed her quiet guest. "What's the matter, dear? Don't you like spaghetti?"

Sally nodded yes, but her chin began to quiver.

Daddy leaned over. "Do you feel alright, Sally?"

Again, she nodded, but now her eyes began to fill with water. She looked pleadingly at her sister. Carol looked at her questioningly, but when Sally didn't say anything, she shrugged and went back to her dinner.

Mother put down the baby's spoon. "What's the matter, honey? Why aren't you eating?" Suddenly, Sally was embarrassingly sobbing into her napkin. Startled eyes looked at her from around the table. Mother pushed back her chair, came around the table and gently led Sally back into the lovely, dark living room.

"Tell me what's wrong. Why are you crying?" Mother asked, sitting the child down on the velvet sofa and kneeling beside her.

Sally gulped, hiccupped and wiped her eyes. She still hadn't said a word.

"Sally, what is it?" Mother demanded softly.

In a small, sad voice, the little girl replied, "Mommy, I don't have a fork."

I wish I could say I learned a lesson that day that stayed with me the rest of my life. I wish I could say that remembering what a ridiculous mountain I made out of such a small pile of spaghetti taught me forever the value of speaking my own mind. I wish I could say I never again waited for someone else to put into words what I was thinking.

Wishing, though, has never been a powerful force in the universe. Wouldn't it be nice, if it were? No more being left behind with pounding heart and sweaty palms, as a conversation gallops off and away from the words you'd practiced so they'd come out right. Am I alone in this? My sister says every little thing that comes into her head and people love her, probably because they can't help but know her.

The individual I became...well, am still becoming...isn't as verbal as she might be. I've lived other embarrassing moments when I kept silent instead of speaking up. It's one of those hard lessons of life—you don't get the spaghetti when you haven't asked for a fork.

Sally Dexter-Smith
Chula Vista, California

Meeting your needs requires that you communicate your needs to others. As this story so aptly points out, if you do not speak up for yourself nobody else will.

We have all encountered people who crush our spirits. You will contribute to the balance of the universe's energy once you overcome negativity to the point where you can avoid responding in anger.

Avoid gossiping about others. It is unhelpful and will negatively influence your self-esteem.

You may not be able to work through issues with everybody. You need to set boundaries and walk away, but it is up to you to do this in as positive a manner as possible. It is self-destructive to discuss issues with someone, if it leaves you feeling bad about what you said or how you shared your message.

Tao Shin Do, or Truthful Pathway

Early in life, I experienced an indiscretion of trust and personal safety and committed to never allowing it to happen again. Due to my proficiency as a martial artist, it has not.

The notion of transforming opposition through love was a concept introduced to me during my martial arts training in San Diego in 1995 and ran counter to most of my traditional training. The use of strength, force and power to defeat one's opponent were the martial mantras that I had previously embraced.

I was concurrently participating in a two-year service of retreats that provided an introduction to various yoga traditions that emphasized a physical and mental cleansing process.

As my martial arts training progressed, I began to observe inconsistencies with truth teachings through my Sensei's talk and actions. However, I intuitively knew that I was walking my path.

My training required participation in tournaments at which I prevailed in competition. These events, while serving as a measure of proficiency, were also inflating my ego.

During this time, I became a Reiki practitioner and began participating in a weekly healing clinic. This practice resulted in a heightened sensitivity to energy, both positive and negative.

The Test

One evening while walking in downtown San Diego, I was offered drugs to which I responded in a manner that offended and angered the drug dealer. His verbal and physical posture clearly conveyed that he was intent on responding to my disrespectful comment.

The true path of the martial artist is to transform opposition through love. I was provided with an opportunity to test this premise and time seemed to suspend while we verbally jousted, parried and deflected energetic blows. Then, a visual softening occurred with my opponent.

He shared that he had just been released from prison and dealing drugs was all that he could do. I assured him that life offers many more options. I reassured him that God cares and provides for His children. He suddenly pulled out a pocket bible and referenced a favorite scripture.

The aggressive opposition expressed by this man had been overcome by love.

As we smiled, wished each other well and embraced, I experienced an intense energy pulse between us. I realized I had let my guard down. I didn't know what had happened. Although I sensed that my interaction with this man was for good, something felt out of sorts.

A Call To God

Later that evening, I awoke to intense abdominal pain in the location where I had sensed the energy pulse. I began vomiting copious amounts of blood. I sensed my life force draining. At that moment, my body became infused with a warm healing Reiki energy, which is the love of God. During this time, I experienced the vision that is recounted in the story provided earlier in this book entitled *Divine By Design*.

The following morning, I awakened in a weak and exhausted state. Within one-half hour of bathing and drinking water, I experienced no further ill effects.

In the following weeks, my relationship with my Sensei began to deteriorate. This resulted in a challenge by him for me to defend my authority to question his actions. I assured him that my newfound confidence would prevail in defending myself by relying on techniques of true self-defense versus self-defeat. My clarity was based on the realization that true self-defense has no relation to the ego based self-defeat of traditional martial arts. The truthful pathway of Tao Shin Do again proved superior to the aggressive nature of my teacher with misguided intention and I continued with my training toward becoming a Sensei.

Although I eventually attained a life long quest, I knew that with the clarity of my life purpose I could not serve two masters. I have renounced violence and discontinued training to attain higher rank as a martial artist. I will always come to the aid of the weak and defenseless, but will come from a place of service through love.

Robert G. Wertz
Divine by Design
www.robert-wertz-design.com
San Diego, California

When you are evaluating your relationships and support system, be aware of which relationships are most conducive to self-discovery. Do the people with whom you spend time support you in who you want to be, or do they want or pressure you to be somebody else? The more comfortable you feel about your decisions, the less others will challenge you. You do not need to state that you are confident. They will know by your behavior. When our family and friends sense our indecisiveness and insecurity this makes them more fearful and anxious, particularly if we are trying to gain their approval. This portrays lack of confidence in what we are doing and encourages others to provide advice or criticism.

Is there a time in your life when you thought you were moving in the direction you wanted, but have since given up your ideals? If you sacrificed them, it may be because the people in your life did not inspire you to continue to pursue your dreams. Messages you received from people in the past may even be inhibiting you now because the tape running in your head says that what you want is unacceptable or you are non-deserving. Life is now something that is simply happening to you. Are you letting others tell you who to be? Are you letting somebody rob you of the self-confidence to stand up for yourself?

Being in control of yourself and your life means doing what you want, not what someone else wants you to do, nor rebelling and doing the opposite to prove a point. Either way, this does not represent freedom. Rebellion represents a negative spiral. It is necessary to reclaim your life and do what you want one step at a time to develop a positive spiral.

You do not do people a favor by constantly sacrificing your needs. It is essential to compromise or take turns in getting needs met in a relationship. When a difference of opinion about what to do arises, determine for which of you it is most important. Take a stand on the ones that count the most. This will lead to more respect, more equality and less resentment. You must be able to count on yourself to make sure your needs are met.

Inspiriters

*You deserve to be around people who value you
and do not judge or manipulate you.*

These people inspire you to accomplish the things you value most in life. They genuinely want for you whatever will make you happiest, even if it is not what they would have chosen. They believe in you.

It is great to be around people who acknowledge your experiences and validate you. I appreciate it when I let somebody know about a mistake I have made and, instead of acting like they think I am an idiot, they say they did that or something similar and we can both laugh at ourselves. "Me, too" experiences contribute greatly to building a relationship. I also like it when someone provides reassurance that lots of people have done the same. It is a relief when I receive genuine reassurance that my mistake was not particularly noticeable because of other things I did at the same time.

People who are spiritually enlightened often prefer to spend time with other like-minded individuals. Develop relationships with people who are also committed to nurturing their souls and not crushing yours.

In positive, supportive and loving relationships both people take responsibility for maintaining the relationship. They treat each other with respect. They are genuinely interested in each other's lives and each is happy when things go well for the other. If some time passes between contact, when they get together it is as if they were never apart. Inspiriters are not only willing to listen to you, but share their vulnerability, too. In order to live a life of abundance, these are the people with whom you need to spend more time.

Intimate Couple Relationships

Are you looking for a romantic relationship? It is when you least need a relationship that you make the best relationship decisions. I recommend you write a list of the characteristics you would value in a long-term intimate relationship. Once these characteristics are in writing, save them. After you meet someone and get to know him/her, review your list. Does this person match? Do not settle for less.

I was a single parent for twelve years. Some of my friends thought my expectations were too high. But, I knew I needed a mate who would be both a good husband and father. I wrote myself a list of desired characteristics including kind, considerate, good sense of humor, enjoys life, intelligent, open, values fitness, and self-motivated. That was my visualization. I finally met a man with those characteristics and we married.

What are you doing to belong? Do you reach out and take risks, or do you expect others to make all the moves. What do you do to make your relationships real? Do you allow yourself to be vulnerable? Do you participate and share yourself?

If you feel desperate for a relationship, you may get one, but it will not be worth having. Devote yourself instead to enjoying life and feeling good about yourself. Building in things to enjoy in life can, in itself, attract good people to you. Having a relationship will not make you whole. You need to become whole before you become involved. You may do this by learning how to meet your own needs through a variety of activities and relationships, and developing as many positive spirals as possible.

It is harmful to try to feel whole through one person, as he/she cannot possibly meet all of your needs, nor can you meet his/hers. Both members in a relationship need to have a good sense of self and share a healthy connection with the universe. This enables them to share a healthy relationship and be less likely to become involved in power struggles.

We have all met people who are desperate to be liked. Being responsible for somebody else's happiness and sense of wellbeing is an impossible burden. It is much easier and pleasurable to spend time with those who are assuming responsibility for making themselves content. They are enthusiastic and charged about life. Time with them is a joy, as their enthusiasm is contagious. And because they are striving to live the life they want to live, they have lots to talk about.

Immediately following my divorce, when I was in my mid-twenties a co-worker told me I was always complaining and did not talk positively about anything. I panicked and ran to see my counselor. I told her I was not upset because my co-worker said I was negative. What upset me was that she was right. As a working single mother of two children under the age of three, my life was tedious. I had already enrolled in college, though, and my counselor reassured me that I would soon have lots of interesting topics to discuss. Pursuing a degree to enable me to become a counselor was my first huge step in making my life one I wanted to live. It was the beginning of a whole new lifestyle. At that time, it was the best thing I could have done for my children and myself. It helped me to develop a pleasant routine, provided the opportunity to meet people and, most importantly, gave me a worthwhile goal.

We are living in an era where it is more difficult to develop healthy relationships. In previous generations, inequality was assumed, abuse was rampant and hardly anybody questioned it. Now, women have more rights and so do children. The rules have changed and most of us have not had effective models. At a time when we are expected to have more equality in our intimate relationships, most men and women have not been shown how to achieve this.

We are all pioneers trying to forge our way
and we must because the rules have changed.

Compromise is a key ingredient for healthy relationships. An essential element to gaining cooperation during negotiation is to ensure that, as much as is humanly possible, you leave the other person's pride intact.

Everybody, no matter how objectionable his or her behavior, has at least one redeeming quality. Find out what it is and keep that in mind during your interactions. It will help you to be more respectful, even while setting boundaries and limits with him/her.

For Terry's Sister

I woke up Wednesday morning with an impending feeling of death. As the morning went on, the feeling brewed and became heavier and heavier. My job involved carrying a sign for a living—one that promoted cigarettes. This was not a great job for a man, but it put food on the table. I was starting my workday at 9:50 a.m. I looked up to God and asked him, "What do you want me to do?"

God said, "Drop the sign. Never pick it up again and go to the funeral at El Camino Mortuary."

I said, "I've got 1/8 tank of gas and only a twenty dollar bill on me. I need to work. I don't have enough fuel to get there."

He said, "She'll make it—round trip."

"What's the quickest way?"

"Clairemont Drive, 5 North, 52 East to Mira Mesa Blvd.—east to Scranton St., follow until you come up to the mortuary—then you will find Terry's funeral."

I followed His directions, but made a wrong turn and took Ardath Road instead of 52 East. Time was running out. It was 10:18 and the service started at 11:00.

I asked for directions again.

"Take a right and go north to La Jolla Village Drive."

I ended up back on the 805, followed directions and arrived with twenty minutes to spare.

Terry was a street person. It seemed everybody in the neighborhood knew him. I had received an intuitive message that I was supposed to be there for Terry's sister so he would have a good turnout to please her. She chaired the funeral.

She asked, "How many of you drank with Terry?"

Everybody's hand went up.

"How many of you gave him money?"

Again, there was a unanimous show of hands.

Terry's sister was surprised and pleased by the turn out for her brother's memorial service. She breathed easier knowing he was finally at rest and no longer struggling.

I'm glad I listened to God. I never picked up that cigarette sign again.

Robert Sexton
Escondido, California

Take the time to get to know friends and family at a more intimate level. Connect with them and talk about things that count. Prepare yourself to be open-minded and non-judgmental. Their thoughts and feelings may be different from yours, but this is acceptable, as you still have your own.

Does your life partner support your vision? Is it compatible with his/hers? Some differences in needs cannot be resolved, such as wanting to live in different countries, unless you are able to frequently travel between the two countries. When one wants to live in a small town or in the country, whereas, the other values city living, you may be able to live in a rural area with access to a city or vice versa. Often, however, this is not financially feasible. If one of you is vegan and the other is not, it may be necessary to prepare more than one main dish at mealtime. Some couples take turns or prepare meals together to avoid the resentment caused by the extra meal preparation. But, for example, if one of you wants children and the other does not, there is no acceptable solution.

Intimacy and satisfaction require mutual sharing. You need to let your partner know what you want or, if you are unsure, at least be able to discuss ideas. Share your dreams. You may think your partner will not understand—but, what if he/she is receptive and you missed out because you did not risk being vulnerable?

Perhaps your relationship is a disaster. You are growing apart and losing respect for each other day by day. Are you sitting back hoping for a miracle? Do you know of anybody who has been rescued from finding a solution for this problem?

It is time to make a choice. You may take steps to improve the situation, or you may end the relationship before the self-esteem you each have left is destroyed.

When taking a look at relationships, it is important to consider the following questions: Do the positives outweigh the negatives? Is there potential for turning things around? If you decide it is worth working on, start small. Notice what you would like to stay the same and what is going well.

Pay close attention to the things he/she does that please you and acknowledge them

This helps to get the downward spiral moving in an upward direction.

If you or your partner feel your relationship is becoming too distant, do something to create more closeness. This may range from giving him/her a compliment, acknowledging something your partner has said or done that pleases you, sharing affection, or arranging to spend time together. If you tend to hesitate in being affectionate, reach out and touch your loved one. Do not wait for him/her to reach out first. Start moving this in a positive direction.

On the other hand, if you or your partner needs some breathing space in the relationship, you could assume responsibility for some distance. Make it possible for your partner to spend time without you. If you feel unable to do this due to lack of trust, you know there are more serious problems and it may be time to seek outside help. Trust is an essential element in any relationship.

When two people start dating, they experiment to discover what is the right amount of closeness and distance in their relationship. Initially, they may be very close, then one of them takes responsibility for distance so the line between them lengthens. Then, one of them assumes responsibility for closeness so the line between them shortens. They go back and forth until they discover the optimal closeness/distance for both of them. In healthy relationships, couples are flexible and take turns assuming responsibility for closeness and distance. If one shortens or lengthens the distance, one or the other eventually resumes the optimal space.

A common unhealthy relationship pattern occurs when one person assumes most of the responsibility for closeness and the other assumes the majority of the responsibility for distance. One person is concerned that the other will engulf him/her; the other worries about abandonment and hangs on tighter. It does not matter which occurs first, it becomes a downward spiral in the relationship.

The only way to mend this is for the one maintaining distance to experiment with assuming responsibility for closeness and the one who maintains the closeness to experiment with assuming responsibility for distance. If both participate in this exercise, trust will gradually build and the relationship will become more balanced.

Relationship Mending Ritual

The following is a homework assignment that goes a long way to mend relationships: Each of you writes a list outlining anything you have ever done to intentionally or unintentionally hurt the other. Do not share this list with each other. Wait one week and meanwhile add to your list as you think of items. Set time aside for the two of you to meet. One of you apologizes for each and every one of the items on your list, while your partner remains silent throughout. Next, it is the other person's turn to apologize for each and every item on his/her list. You only get to do this once, so make it count. When done with good intentions, honesty and integrity, this homework assignment leads to remarkable healing in a relationship.

There is no justifiable reason for two people to stay in a relationship lacking mutual respect and love. If you think you should stay together for the benefit of your children, ask yourself whether these are the relationship qualities you wish to model for your children. If you cannot improve the relationship, separation is preferable. You will be a better person and this is the best role model you can provide your children. Many children have appreciated improved relationships with both of their parents following separation, provided both parents are willing. It takes time to develop, but you can help make it happen.

Regardless of whether or not you have children, if you have tried and you firmly believe there is nothing left that you can do to improve the situation, you do not do your partner a favor by staying with him/her when the relationship leaves you feeling miserable. If you cannot make it work, free him/her and yourself to find a more meaningful existence.

Relationships with Your Children

Some people were disapproving when I decided to attend university. I was a single parent of two boys, aged two and three years. Family life, however, developed a pleasant routine when I became a student and we enjoyed a stronger sense of security and stability. I was a better mother once my life became more meaningful and I became more able to appreciate the time I spent with my children.

Raising children is a huge responsibility. Some children are born with a difficult temperament, which makes parenting extremely challenging. This is particularly difficult in view of the fact that many parents have not been shown acceptable methods to manage children's behavior. Children tend to be spontaneous, fun loving and accepting of others until they are taught otherwise. In your quest to ensure that you respect your children's rights, you may be unsure about how to contribute to their self-esteem and self-confidence, while at the same time setting necessary limits and boundaries.

Throughout my years as a family therapist, there have been several things that have become clear to me in families where the parent(s) are unable to set firm and consistent limits with a child:

- A child does not feel secure unless his parent(s) demonstrate that they can cope with whatever behavior he exhibits. It is absolutely imperative that his behavior be met with a united front between parents, parents and caregivers, and parents and school staff.

- It is too much responsibility and overwhelming for a child to have this much power. This makes him unable to gain a strong sense of self and a clear understanding of personal boundaries.

- He learns that the only time he is safe is when he has absolute control. He/she learns to take control using whatever means possible, such as manipulation and charm; self-pity and crying; and/or verbal and physical aggression.

- Physical discipline escalates the behavior, as the child wins every time he gets a parent to lose control.

- Unless the parent(s) regain control through appropriate behavior management, the child continues to feel insecure, with possessive and controlling behavior. His perception of the severity of his behavior is greatly minimized in his mind. He is able to rationalize or make excuses for almost everything he does.

You must effectively manage your child's behavior and you need to spend quality one-on-one time with him/her. If you are unable to provide firm and consistent limits, I recommend you consult with a professional. If therapy does not go well after you have given it an honest try, change counselors. You must find a counselor who is a good fit for you and your family.

Children need unconditional love and one-on-one time. Nothing contributes to a child's self-esteem as much as quality time with his/her parents. Even 15 minutes each day can make a significant difference. It is a good idea to schedule quality time into your weekly routine to ensure that this occurs. Otherwise, it is too easy to become distracted by other responsibilities.

I read to my two sons every night during their younger years and then spent ten minutes with each one sharing what we called Talk Time. During this time, we chatted about whatever they wanted. I found that if I asked what they did at school that day, I usually received no answer. When I asked more specific questions such as what they did in gym, who they hung out with at recess, what games they played at recess, or what the snack was at the day care, etc. this made it easier for them. Provided you are able to avoid lecturing your child, he/she will soon grow to cherish this time together. If you are careful about not letting him/her convince you to extend the time, it will be manageable for you.

Sunday afternoons were dedicated to outdoor activities such as visiting the zoo, going to parks or skating. We shared Family Fun Night on Friday evenings. The evening activities changed throughout the years. When they were younger, we played board games. In later years, we made homemade pizza and rented a movie. The regularity of Family Fun Night gradually dwindled when they reached the age where they would rather be with their peers. It is developmentally appropriate for children to spend more time with peers and less with parents once they reach adolescence.

I enrolled my sons in soccer when they were ages four and five. They participated in community outdoor soccer each summer and indoor soccer each winter. I attended as many of their games as I could. It was great when they were on the same team, but hard to be in two places at once when they were not. Fortunately, I was able to carpool with the other parents. Once I married my second husband, both sons took paragliding lessons during adolescence. We also enjoyed skiing, golfing and surfing with them during their adult years. It is the common interests you share with your children that last long into adulthood. Never underestimate the importance of the impact you have on your children.

The following story demonstrates the strength of the bond between a father and his son:

A Son's Love

Many years ago, my four-year-old nephew was traveling with his father on their way to a local campground. While on the freeway between their suburban home and the mountains, a truck traveling in the opposite direction was experiencing some trouble. It seems that the owner of the truck had failed to put safety chains on the truck hitch and the airplane trailer that he was towing. At a dip in the freeway, the hitch broke and the very large trailer jackknifed over the freeway median. The trailer landed on the front of the car in which my nephew was traveling and flipped the car over, somersaulting the car across the freeway lanes.

Although my nephew was wearing a seatbelt, the motion of the car twirling through the air sent him sailing out of the car window. When the car finally landed, his father was trapped hanging upside down in the car, his body mortally trapped inside the crushed automobile. My nephew landed sitting in the middle of a busy six-lane freeway without broken bones or bruises. Cars streamed past him on both sides until the traffic came to a screaming halt.

Within a very short time, both my nephew and my brother were whisked to the hospital where my brother later died on the operating table. Much to the surprise of the police, doctors and witnesses at the scene, my nephew had no apparent injuries. He was admitted into the hospital for observation and his electrolyte count was dreadfully off. The doctors decided he needed to stay hospitalized until his count returned to normal.

Five days passed and my nephew's condition did not change. His color, appetite and countenance were totally gray. He lay listless and small in his hospital bed, never smiling or crying, regardless of all the attention and love bestowed upon him. On the sixth day, the doctor asked his mother if she had told my nephew that his father was dead. Not knowing exactly when or how to do this, she had decided not to tell him until he was well enough to hear the news. The doctor believed he needed to know—he probably already knew intuitively and was distressed that nobody was willing to talk about it with him. So she told him. Within twenty minutes, Tommy had regained his previous healthy color, his appetite and his four-year-old rambunctiousness. He was immediately released from the hospital.

Anonymous
El Cajon, California

Seven

Experiment with Leisure Time

If your first reaction is *What leisure time?* you need to remedy the situation.

Many of us tend to give, give, and give some more. Do you remember the old adage about the empty cup? If you keep giving of yourself and emptying your cup out, you need to put back in. You can refill your cup by getting your needs met by yourself or others. You must take care of yourself. This is not selfish. It will enable you to be a better person, parent, partner, sibling, friend and employee. If you assume responsibility for meeting your needs, you will have more to give.

Build in breaks. Listen to your intuition and take time out to do something just because you want to. Let others help you. Accept compliments. Treat yourself well. You need something to look forward to, such as time with special people, being alone, and doing things you enjoy.

I was previously uncomfortable spending time with myself. One of my counselors once told me she felt sorry for my personal telephone book because she knew that as soon as I was alone, I would start peeling through the pages trying to find someone to talk with on the phone. Now, I cherish time alone.

I once called a friend and invited her over for tea. She declined and said, "I'm too lazy."

I was offended. The next time we were together, she revealed that she had refused to visit because she needed to be alone. If only she had said so. I was able to understand her need for time to herself, but being told she was too lazy left me feeling I was not worth the bother.

Stop at a park on the way home from work, or take a shower, bath or brief timeout when you arrive home. Help yourself to get centered after a hectic day at work, so you do not take out your frustrations on loved ones.

One of the special things I do for myself is enjoy a cup of herbal tea in a beautiful crystal etched mug that was given to me as a gift. I like to listen to quiet music accompanied by the sound of birds singing and chirping. Find out what gives you pleasure and do it more often. If you do not build in leisure escapes for yourself, nobody will. Spend quiet time alone and take time to appreciate life.

When you are driving or walking, do you notice the scenery? Are you oblivious to the wonders in your life? Perhaps you could notice them more—maybe even start a gratitude journal.

When developing leisure time, it may be as simple as making room in your life for activities you used to enjoy. Are there any activities you used to do, but are no longer involved in, that you might enjoy now? Is there anything you have wanted to do, but have not done yet? You can leaf through the yellow pages or a community catalog for ideas. Choose at least one activity. It might be a good idea to start with something that does not require a large commitment of time or investment of money unless it is something you already feel fairly certain or passionate about.

Once the time arrives, you may be reluctant to attend. Once there, you will probably be glad you did. If you are not—think about what it was about that activity that was not good for you and use that information to help you choose another activity. Give yourself permission to quit and try something else.

Choose activities that are enough of a distraction that you do not think about your problems. Notice which activities you enjoy most and do them more often.

Challenge yourself. Take courses. Read books that stimulate you, such as self-help or mysteries. Educate yourself through learning about other cultures or trying new recipes. Experiment with bringing more things into your life that interest and appeal to you. See what develops.

How is your physical health? Self-care involves being fit. If you are unhappy about your weight or level of fitness, it may be time to take control of the situation. It will require hard work and determination, with no excuses. It is another positive spiral situation. The better you take care of yourself, the more you will feel good about yourself and the better you feel about yourself the more you will take care of yourself.

If you are waiting to feel better about yourself, you could be waiting a long time. It is the practical concrete things we do that give messages to ourselves that we are deserving and worthy individuals. The more you contribute to your own self-esteem, the more energetic you will be and the more likely to discover personal creativity.

So often we continue to push ourselves and decide we will relax and take time off when a project is complete or well established. Our bodies often do not work on our time clock and, when the stress is finally over, we become ill. Illness is never timely. It is better to take a break in the middle of the stress so your body does not crash when you reach the end of the adrenaline rush. If you do not find time to be healthy, your body will find time to be sick.

Throw on some sneakers and go for a daily walk. You will be surprised at how this reduces stress and replenishes your energy. If your co-workers walk with you, do not talk about work. If you are walking alone, pay attention to your environment. Most importantly—breathe!

You can accomplish great things when your body is unhealthy or unfit, but you will not have the same level of optimism or energy. If you have let things slide in the area of self-care, it is time to reclaim your body for your own. Include fitness, healthy diet and overcoming addictions in your list of goals for yourself. Do not keep it to yourself. Enlist the support of others. Sharing with others may be the beginning of committing yourself to your goals. There is nothing like group or team camaraderie to help encourage you toward success, as demonstrated by the following story:

Revelation

I never thought I was a drunk. Never.

I lived in a wealthy town. Everybody drank or so it seemed to me. The town police knew and liked me. They would call in advance to arrange for an officer to drive me back and forth to parties to ensure that I did not drive while under the influence of alcohol.

I had my own business and money was never a problem. I sold that business, divorced my husband, and relocated to California because education was free provided you were a resident. I wanted my children to pursue post-secondary education. Both ran away from home before they had the chance.

I went to jail on three occasions due to driving under the influence. My driver's license was never withdrawn. The last time I was jailed, I swore I hadn't had more than two drinks. I wrote a check for bail, knowing full well that it would bounce. I planned to kill myself, but somebody honored the check for me. The result of my breathalizer test was a phenomenal 2.8.

I found an attorney who managed to have me admitted to the Lucky Duce program for recovering alcoholics. I was suddenly very aware of how bright-eyed two recovering alcoholics appeared, as they spoke to us of recovery.

While traveling home that same day, just past Camp Pendleton on I-5 where the sun setting on the ocean is a glorious spectacle, my car was suddenly filled with a presence and I felt overwhelmed as the presence enveloped me. I started to cry. *I'm an alcoholic. Finally, I understand the reason behind the mess my life is in. What a relief—I can do something about it.*

I called the Treasurer of the firm where I worked. He was open about the fact that he was a recovering alcoholic and he invited me to visit his home. I was excited about joining Alcoholics Anonymous. My children had run away from home, my pets had died, I was in trouble, and there was a name for my problem.

I'm a fighter, I'm feisty and I'm very energetic. On top of that, I have always believed in a Higher Power that would support me with my challenges. I have been sober for more than 29 years now. I'm so glad I saw the light before it was too late.

Anonymous
Encinitas, CA

Your soul will thrive through self-awareness and self-acceptance. Self-denigrating thoughts and comments attack your personal essence. It is up to you to feed and nurture your soul. Make sure you avoid beating yourself up for slipping. Instead, get yourself back on track, as quickly as you can. This is what works—this is what feels good.

Body pain often indicates we are either ruminating about the past or worrying about the future.

It is important to live in the present and our bodies let us know when we are not. If you are somebody who constantly ruminates about the past, experiment with bringing new activities into your life. Do things that consume and distract you enough that you are in the present. If you find yourself constantly striving to grasp your future, experiment with appreciating the here and now. Again, notice which activities distract you best and do them more often.

If you focus on the future, you will feel frustrated. After you reach each goal, you will plan another. This is what makes life interesting and challenging. You are where you need to be right now at this very minute. One minute from now, you will be in a new position. We cannot delete experience. We can appreciate it now, while it is happening and then, a new position will be here for us to experience and hopefully savor.

Likewise, it is important to appreciate the developmental stages, even when they provide unpleasant challenges.

Many years ago, my previous husband and I decided to replace our waterbed mattress. We picked out a foam mattress and box spring, paying twenty dollars to have them delivered. I woke that night hot and soaking wet. One of my friends suggested that maybe it was due to the foam mattress, so we paid twenty dollars to have it returned to the store and paid another twenty dollars to have a coil mattress delivered. I again woke in the middle of night soaking wet. We paid another twenty dollars to have that set returned to the store and re-installed our waterbed mattress. My twin sister called that evening and mentioned that when she had visited her physician that afternoon he had diagnosed her as peri-menopausal.

"How did he know?" I asked.

"I was having night sweats."

People rarely find menopause humorous, but I have had more than a chuckle or two over this experience.

You need to be involved in your day-to-day life, rather than spending time dwelling on the past or expecting things in the future. What totally absorbs you to the point where you forget about time and whatever is going on around you? Being in the present does not mean giving up on your future. Enjoy what you are doing now and your future will unfold regardless.

Many people are being diagnosed with invisible conditions such as fibromyalgia and chronic fatigue syndrome. This is often an indication that a person is carrying around past hurt and other people's energy in their space, which leads to physical ailments. Cleansing rituals where you ground and run energy can be very helpful in removing other people's energy from your space. One of the benefits of meditation is that it brings you into the here and now. Meditation is the single most important thing you can do to nurture your soul.

When you discover your soul—
this is when you become free.

If you are ill or injured, give your body adequate time to recover. For example, sore throats encourage us to drink more fluids to help cleanse germs. Coughing and runny noses are two of the ways our body works to naturally eliminate germs. Let your body's natural healing do its job.

If your body is speaking to you, are you listening? Your body tells you what you need. If you are tired, you need more rest. You should be able to wake each morning without an alarm clock. If not, you are not getting enough sleep. If you have tension headaches, shoulder/neck pain or stomach pain related to stress, you need more relaxation. If you constantly feel hungry, you may need more nutrition. If you feel thirsty, you are already dehydrated. Drink water frequently throughout the day. Lethargy indicates you need more to anticipate. What can you do to make your body complain less about your life?

Sexual intercourse in a mutually caring relationship contributes to your own personal health and also contributes to the health of loving intimate relationships. Orgasms release natural endorphins, which diminish pain and combat depression.

Many people suffer from depression at some time in their lives and some more than others. You may feel pressured to overcome your depression by those around you, yourself or both. Depression is a message that something is not working well in your life. It is also a message from your body that you need to rest. You have to give yourself permission to do less until you are ready to get on with your life. Telling yourself you cannot be depressed only prolongs the inevitable.

If you are going through a crisis, your body tends to get stuck in the fight or flight syndrome. This produces extra adrenaline to help you to rise to the challenge. Anytime you relax, eat, or sleep, it fools your body into thinking the crisis is over. This produces less adrenaline, which in turn helps you to relax, sleep, and eat. What you want to do is get the spiral going in this direction.

Depression is a temporary state, which only feels like it will last forever, particularly if you have experienced it before and recovery was lengthy. The advantage to having worked your way out once is that you know you can do it again.

There is often a connection between being depressed and feeling overwhelmed. At one point, I realized I was cringing every time I opened my business email account because I felt overextended and worried about more demands on my time. For me, this was an indication that I needed to get organized again and take some time for myself.

I did and this helped me to become ready to reach out to the media again and welcome their interest in interviewing me.

Develop more realistic expectations of yourself. If I were to write a list of things I could do to promote my books, it would be infinite and impossible to accomplish. I choose a few methods each week and ignore the rest.

Write a list of things to do, do the top priority tasks and leave the rest to the universe.

If you are depressed, rest up as much as you can until you are ready to tackle the world again. Although a crisis may make you fearful, it also brings the opportunity for change. It is more than coincidence that the Chinese symbol for crisis combines the symbols of danger and opportunity.

Listen to depression's message. Withdraw from life somewhat until you are ready to make change, then start to take control again. The best way to escape depression is to do something else. What does depression look like for you? For most people, it involves inactivity. You do not feel like getting up, making decisions, or doing activities that previously provided enjoyment. This is how you *do* depression—you do not do much of anything.

If you do not want to do depression— you need to do something else.

Introduce more spontaneity into your life. Make some out of the blue decisions, such as sharing affection, making a phone call to someone you care about, going for a walk, or stopping to smell the roses. Being organized in terms of knowing where things are when you need them and planning your work schedule are important, but this should provide more time for spontaneity, not less.

Develop a plan for how you are going to get your day started and follow it. Some people find starting the day with exercise to be helpful. I would not think of recommending exercise unless this is something you think would work for you. It is acceptable to think smaller, as long as it gets you going. This is something you can take control of yourself. If you give this a good try and you are still feeling depressed, you may consider consulting with a physician.

The more you do, the more you are capable of doing. Have you ever noticed that you can get lots done in a short period of time, but if you have more time available it will take you longer to accomplish the same tasks? It is, of course, important to follow this premise within reason. The key word is balance.

If you are an agitated, depressed person who spends life running around, doing countless busy activities to avoid being alone with yourself, it is time to do something different. It is time for less hustle and bustle and more meaningful activity. How about discovering something to enjoy in your life? Make your schedule manageable. Build in breaks for yourself.

Are you experiencing difficulty making decisions? Have you tried writing a pros and cons list? It is amazing how visually reviewing choices brings clarity. The following is an example from *Time To Heal* when the main character was trying to decide whether to re-mortgage her house or sell to purchase a smaller, less expensive home after her husband left:

Re-mortgage House

Pros	*Cons*
Don't have to move	*Higher payments*
Avoid stress of selling	*Huge-higher utilities*
Showy	*More housework*
Spacious	*Associated with Ted*

Buy Smaller House

Pros	*Cons*
Lower payments	*Have to move*
Smaller—less utilities	*Not as new*
Less housework	*Less space*
Cozy	
New beginning	

It was clear to her. She was going to have to list their house for sale and find a smaller house nearby.

Regardless of how difficult the situation is, it is hard to leave what is familiar. Take baby steps, meanwhile telling yourself you can do it. You are just as good and deserving as anybody. With each success, it will become easier to believe in yourself.

It helps to think about people or characters you admire and respect. What would they do in this situation? Maybe this is a solution for you.

I make sure I eat nutritiously, get adequate rest and build in breaks for myself to ensure optimal work performance because I have messed up often enough to have a clear idea of what I need. This is something you need to know about yourself, too.

Reward yourself for your accomplishments.

It does not matter whose life it is, everyone has unpleasant tasks. There is absolutely no reason why you cannot reward yourself for getting them done. For example, if you do not feel like cleaning up after dinner, calling your insurance agent, or changing the car oil, tell yourself you may do something you want to do if you get it done by a certain time. Promise yourself you can do something enjoyable, such as watch your favorite television program, read a chapter in a book, call a special friend or go for a walk.

Reward yourself for making a phone call you have been dreading or taking care of business, i.e. lawyer, banking, etc.—whatever is involved.

With respect to tasks, avoid dragging them out. Set some time aside to do more than one and then reward yourself when you are done. Try to be realistic to avoid setting yourself up for failure. You can accomplish fantastic things a bit at a time.

Simplify your life. It is best to set deadlines for short-term goals. Decide the best time to do it and plan for it. This makes things more manageable and helps you to be in control. When unexpected events occur that interfere, reschedule it for a later time.

Everything negative is magnified when you are tired.
Be kind to yourself and take breaks when needed.

Self-care contributes to self-esteem. It not only helps you feel better about yourself, but also gives you the message that you count and are worthy. Do something special for yourself and do something special for somebody else. Both will feel great and it could be the beginning of another positive spiral.

Spend time alone—take time to reflect and/or meditate.

Where do you go to re-group? Can you arrange to go there soon? If you do not have a sanctuary, can you make a special place for yourself?

If you want to discover what you need in life, you must spend time searching your soul, which involves spending time alone. In what ways do you nurture your soul? This may include appreciation of food, the work you do, beauty, art, culture, history, relationships, creativity, time alone, peacefulness or developing a sense of belonging.

Do you tend to spend a lot of time worrying? If so, you might find it helpful to set up a worry schedule. When my first marriage dissolved, I was receiving counseling from two female co-therapists. My counselors noted that I was spending a lot of time worrying —in my car on the way to work, anytime I was not busy at my job, while I was cooking, etc. When they first suggested that I schedule my worry time, I thought they were insane.

They said that if I was going to worry, I might as well do a good job and I should set some time aside for worrying. They asked me to choose one-half hour each day. I chose 10:00 to 10:30 p.m. after my children were asleep and my homework was complete. They said I should take the time to worry, no matter where I was or whether it was convenient. It was important to make the time available, so that if I caught myself worrying during the day I could tell myself to save it until later. I was asked to have a pen and paper handy to write down my problems and any ideas that came to mind. If I could not last the full day without worrying, I could have one-half hour after lunch.

I thought it was a ridiculous idea. However, I learned an invaluable lesson. I soon discovered I did not need one-half hour after lunch to worry and there were more enjoyable things to do. I became very effective at problem solving in the brief time I set aside in the evening. It became easy to put off worrying during the day because I knew I would take care of things later. If I caught myself worrying outside of the scheduled time, I would ask myself, *What is good about right now?* I could restrict my worry time and it made the rest of the day much more pleasant.

Do you need to set up a schedule to contain your worrying? You might as well make good use of the time and do some constructive problem solving. You cannot do this if you are doing other things at the same time. You may come up with some ideas that are a start toward resolving the problem. You may even decide to take action and in this way give yourself more control.

If you feel your life is out of control, you may have contemplated ending it.

Nothing is ever so bad that you do not have
at least one more acceptable option other than suicide.

As a client pointed out to me many years ago, you can always go live as a *bum* on the beach in Mexico. There were times in my life that I liked knowing I had another option. You also have another option. Make your life one worth living.

A childhood friend who overdosed on drugs and drowned during adolescence came to visit me from the other side. He said it is important for my readers to know that there are two tunnels in the spirit world, a tunnel of darkness and one of light. Regardless of whether or not a person ends his own life, he has the option of choosing the light. Those who don't, may be brought to the light at a later date.

I'm Okay...I'm Fine

"I'm okay," she said. "I'm strong. I deal with the stuff. I'm fine." She hung up the phone. "I'm fine."

She felt the numbness. Sure, she was fine. She couldn't feel anymore. *Who wants to feel?* A marriage of four decades gone...she was alone...still pining over the abusive relationship...while he found a new love.

Sure, she's fine. Then, there's her son...dying, alienated from the family. She didn't know where he was or how he was. She was alienated from her other children. Sure, she's fine. The walls were closing in. It was getting dark. Finances...Where was she going to live? How was she going to live? "I'm fine," she said. The darkness was getting very comfortable.

It didn't really matter anymore..."I'm fine."...the words were hollow and dull. I'm fine. Her world was upside down. The dream turned into a nightmare. I'm fine. It's getting darker and darker. She feels the peace. No more worries ...No more talking...No more...of one more time of pulling herself out of the hole. I'm fine. I'm fine. Slipping away, slipping away...going quietly in her sleep. No one would notice...no one would miss her.

Her father would never know. He wouldn't call to check on her, and no one would call him to tell him. Then, there were the aunts, uncles, cousins. They wouldn't know either...*No one cared,* she thought. *They won't even notice.* Her children, they wouldn't notice either...her friends, maybe. But they'd get over it. She'd been a burden to them. Quietly, quietly, she would go away...the light that tried so hard to shine through...finally went out...

She closed her eyes and began to sleep. Her breath became shallow and gradually there were fewer and fewer breaths...until...

She felt something near her. Something touched her. She felt a presence. She heard a voice. "I am here. You are not alone. I will notice. I love you."

She didn't want anyone there. Finally, she found peace. "No," she screamed. "Let me go. The pain is too much. I cannot go on. Let me go..."

Gently, lovingly, the voice said, "I love you. It is not time. I have work for you to do. You are loved by many. They need you."

"No," she said. "No, I cannot go on. I have too many losses. I have too much pain. I cannot bear this alone. Nooooooo..."

"I know your pain. I know your losses. You are not alone. I am here, and I was always there...loving you, holding you, caressing you. Holding you up when you could not go on."

"I have a beautiful future planned for you...an exciting adventure. You are my beloved daughter, and I will not abandon you. I love you. I know you. You cannot hide from me. I know your deepest, darkest secrets; and I love you. I love you just the way you are."

"You see, I know your heart; and I know your soul. You are my prize. I adore you. I know that one day you will see the beauty of your soul and the love in your heart. You do have a purpose. You are fulfilling it right now. Each time that you fall and get back up, you get stronger. You do this not only for yourself, but for others...your friends, your children. They see you. They notice. They are watching you. What do you want them to see? Who do you want to be?"

"Remember this…if you can remember only one thing, remember this…I love you. Baby, what do you want?"

She was drifting deeper. She didn't want to hear. She didn't want to come back. It was so peaceful. *Just let me go,* she thought.

The still, quiet voice said very softly, "I love you…No…"

Tears began to stream down her cheeks. She felt her breath. She felt the light inside her. She felt its warmth.

"What am I going to do?" She wept. "What am I going to do?"

The voice said, "You are going to live. Live joyfully. Live each day, so that others know who I am…"

She opened her eyes and smiled. She knew that she was not alone. She knew that she was loved. She knew that someone would notice. She knew that she could live a joyful life. She felt a different kind of peace as she remembered…

God's gift to us is life. Our gift to God is how we live it.

Anonymous
Encinitas, California

Eight

Consider What Your Home Means to You

Does it feel good to return home? Are you proud to bring people there? If not, what could you do to make it more pleasant? Is it time to move?

You may need to let go in the faith that the universe will make things happen for you, as shown in the following story from my sister, Karen:

Creative Intervention

Linda and I attended the same schools as my husband, Rick, and we also grew up with his best friend, Mark. Mark, however, passed on in a motor vehicle accident when he was 21 years old. Mark often came to visit Linda from the other side and he told her that he had helped Rick to design and build each of our homes.

We had recently been busy looking for new property, either to purchase a pre-built home or build our own. Mark had asked Linda to tell Rick to stop looking at pre-built homes, as they were going to build another home together. Rick, however, had continued looking.

I was becoming stressed, with all of the other demands in my life on top of the uncertainty around purchasing new property. Linda suggested I write down all of the characteristics I wanted in a house and property and ask my angels for it, so I did.

One day later, for the first time, I invited my friend, Shirley, to walk with me. Shirley was expecting to visit another friend that day and was waiting to hear back from her. We took my dog for a walk for an hour and then checked Shirley's email from my computer. She also checked her voice mail. There was no message from her friend, so we decided to spend the morning together.

Shirley mentioned that she had noticed a property for sale in a district where my husband and I were interested. The sign had only been up for a day. She suggested that she and I drive by the property. I was very impressed and left a message with my realtor to schedule a viewing. I knew within minutes of entering the house that this was the property I wanted. Despite all of the properties my husband and I had viewed, it was the first home to excite me.

The next day, Shirley's friend told her that she had sent a message by email asking her to visit, but the message was kicked back—despite having used the correct email address. Mark later told Linda he had located this property for us because he knew Rick wasn't going to give up and I needed more security and stability. He said he had bounced the email, so Shirley would have the opportunity to show the property to me before it sold as properties in the area were selling in less than one or two days.

Karen Nelson
Qualicum Beach, British Columbia

Are you living in the environment that is most conducive to your desired lifestyle? If you are a person who loves water, it does not make sense to live in the desert. Where do you want to live? What does it look like? How does it sound? What are you doing? Who will you interact with? What would you miss, if you were living there as compared to where you are currently living? Consider weather, culture, work, leisure activities and people.

When I completed my Masters Degree, I was a single parent. There was a hiring freeze in Calgary, the city where I lived, and also in Edmonton, the only other large city in my home province of Alberta. I had two children, ages 10 and 11, to support and a huge decision to make. I chose to relocate to a small town in northeastern Alberta. The job did not turn out. For liable reasons, I will not explain what was happening in management, but six months later I took the first counseling position that came up in Edmonton and relocated my children again. It was another nine months before we were able to return to Calgary.

My parents continued to live in the same home that I grew up in since age two. Moving was a significant event for me and I had lots of misgivings about uprooting my children. On the other hand, I later realized that I had given them a gift. They discovered they could start over in an entirely new community and school. These moves contributed to their self-confidence in a way that living in the same community for their entire childhood never could have done. I am not recommending that you uproot your family just to give them practice, but taking risks and succeeding gives us confidence.

Not only did I gain incredible experience in those two jobs, I also developed my self-confidence. There were few resources available in either of those counseling positions and I had the opportunity to discover how capable I was. I learned I could survive in a new environment without any familiar supports. I had to create new friendships and I found out which of my relationships in Calgary were most meaningful to me. This experience added personal tools for my sons and myself that can be used again.

We each have our own personal bag of tools that have worked in the past and can be used over and over again. Are you making sure that you use yours?

Many people think that, if they move, most of their problems will go away. Geographical cures do not work unless you do something different following the move. I thought moving to a rural town would reduce stress and help me slow down. What I needed at that point in my life was to discover the importance of building in more leisure time. That discovery could have been made, no matter where I lived. If you can change yourself in the old circumstances, you can take the new you to a different situation and things will be different.

If you are moving to avoid a relationship, you will probably recreate a similar relationship in the new location. Because we attract what we fear, the same problem arises repeatedly until we respond differently and effectively.

Are you learning from your mistakes or just recycling them? This is essential in both the small and large areas of life. I had to keep learning from my mistakes when it came to marketing my book. I discovered just before closing time at a book fair that people did not come over because they assumed my book was too expensive. Since then, I have always posted a sign advertising the price. I handed out over 100 bookmarks at Bookexpoamerica, but did not realize that it was not obvious that I was the author and that I needed to tell people. I distributed hundreds of flyers advertising my book on sidewalks near bookstores in the San Diego area before I discovered that it would be advantageous to mention that the story was set in the San Diego locale. Unfortunately, I could not go back and do it right, but I could change what I did in the future.

Clutter Attacking

Get rid of clutter and make your life more manageable. Clutter distracts us from things that matter in our lives and tends to leave us feeling overwhelmed. Clearing out mess makes room for flow of energy in your personal space and life, helping you to feel more in control. Getting rid of old energy provides space for opportunities to come into your life.

If you have not used it in the past year—you are not going to—get rid of it. If it is not a seasonal item and you have not used it in the past six months—get rid of it. If it brings an automatic smile to your face or feeling of longing or helps you recall a fond memory—find a place for it.

I also recommend that you tackle one area at a time. It might be as small as a shelf in a cupboard or one drawer, an area of the closet, or an area in a room or garage.

Do not tear your home apart in one clutter organizing frenzy.

Mass clutter attacking can soon become extremely overwhelming. If you are interrupted or become disheartened midstream, you will be left living in a disaster area. If you prefer, you can toss a few items every time you think of it.

I attended a seminar when I was in my early twenties with a couple of hundred other women who worked in clerical positions in the Calgary Board of Education. There was a lunchtime speaker who talked to us about the various personality types. She explained that our individual personalities govern the way we dress and how we walk. She suggested we go through our closets and notice which clothes contributed to our self-confidence.

Most of us have a collection of clothes because they were in fashion, the price was right or somebody else thought we looked good in them. If you want to feel confident and free, you need to wear clothes that help you feel good and this applies to both men and women. Open your closet right now and throw out a few of the items you do not like. It does not matter if it is because they're uncomfortable, the color is wrong or the style is not you. Honor yourself and get rid of them.

What do the clothes you feel good in have in common? Keep this in mind next time you are shopping. I often used to buy clothes that needed to be altered or ones I wished were a little bit different. I avoid making purchases now unless my first thought upon trying them on is, *This was made for me.*

Bodies are just bodies. They say nothing about who you are as a person—your inner self. The image and messages you want to project are, *I feel good* and *I deserve to feel good.* Wear the clothes that help you feel comfortable and confident. Let people know who you are.

Clutter attacking is a perfect positive procrastination activity. Positive procrastination is something you do that you do not want to do because it saves you from doing something else you really, really do not want to do—like preparing taxes. Give yourself permission to participate in positive procrastination.

Garage sales can be arduous tasks. They tend to be time-consuming and not generally worth the money unless you enjoy them or are selling large items. It is sometimes quicker to pack up everything and give it to a local charity or call one for pick up. You may even request a receipt for income tax purposes, which in some cases may more than cover the amount you would have made in a garage sale.

When you feel bad about throwing out an item that is in good condition, give it to someone who will use it. If you do not know anybody who would benefit, give it to a charity.

If you are storing other people's belongings, you may return or throw them out. Ask the person to pick up the items, let him know that he has until a certain date and then

162

you will be giving them to charity. Make sure you follow through. If he wanted them bad enough he would have met your deadline.

After we sold almost all of our household belongings and moved into our recreational vehicle, it felt incredibly freeing to get rid of that much clutter in one fell sweep. I will never be a collector now that I know how good it feels to only keep essentials.

When we were threatened by fire in San Diego and thought we might have to evacuate at short notice, I was surprised by the limited number of items we felt the need to take with us. My husband downloaded the hard drive of the computer onto a CD and we put photo albums, toiletries and a box of files by the door. The only other things I intended to take out were my purse, a change of clothes and my Betta fish in his fishbowl.

Ensure that when you decorate your home, you leave room for what designers refer to as negative space. This includes blank wall and empty space on the tables, shelves or counter, which promotes energy flow and feelings of calm.

A small change can be uplifting. Change one thing or introduce one new item to your home. Even exchanging pictures or rearranging the furniture will be noticeable.

Organize Your Life

Get your life in order. What do you need to take care of to free you to get on with your life?

If you have unfinished business nagging you,
tackle tasks one by one.

It is draining to put off chores. You will be better off once you get them done and over with. This leads to feelings of relief, makes your priorities more obvious and helps reveal your passions and dreams. It will lead to increased space and energy in your life. More importantly, it will open up space for good things to come in.

If the task you need to tackle is large and you feel overwhelmed, break it down and handle each piece one at a time.

Feeling guilty about your lack of accomplishment depletes the energy you could be using to get things done. There is a sense of pride upon completion and a feeling of relief that can be energizing. If you are a person who likes to write lists, you can list the items that are nagging you and check them off. This system may not be beneficial, if you tend to admonish yourself for not getting more done. Instead, you may find it helpful to keep a list of tasks you have completed to encourage you and provide you with a sense of accomplishment.

Pay close attention to the wondrous things that happen, as you clear the path for things that count. They will start coming to you before you know it.

Take care of financial matters. If you have accrued considerable debt and you have been hoping things will get better with time, you have probably noticed that they have not. Earning more money can help provide financial relief, but spending less is usually more effective. In what areas can you cut back? If you usually buy lunch, could you pack a lunch and eat out only one day per week? Could you get CD's and movies from the library instead of renting or buying them? Are you able to give up smoking or switch to rolling your own? Could you purchase snacks and sodas at the supermarket instead of using vending machines? Consider the things you do without questioning the cost. Maybe there is something you could do differently to reduce regular expenditures.

Create a positive spiral through spending less and having more control over your finances. If this will not make the difference, are you able to request a raise in salary or temporarily assume an additional part-time job to get your head above water? You need to manage your finances well to invite abundance into your life.

When things are stressful, being organized and in control at home and at my desk helps to give me a sense of calm. Whether you are in the workplace or at home, you may find it helpful to list tasks. Notes can occupy one or two piles instead of being spread all over, or they can be compiled into one list of things to do. It may be helpful to prioritize or list them according to when they need to be done.

If there is lots of background noise and you have the option, replace it with music or sounds of nature. You will hear it at a subconscious level and it will help calm you.

If you work with or for someone who brings chaos into your life, build in order wherever you can and build in breaks for yourself, such as lunchtime walks, sitting in the park, reading outside or in your car, or meditating. Find something that distracts you from thinking about work.

Nine

Get Yourself Ready for Big Things to Happen

You may think about people you know who are successful and say to yourself, *They are different than me. They are outgoing. I could never be like that. They are strong. I am not. They have money. I do not.* How did they get there or become that way? Most of them were not born this way, but developed the skills and assets they needed to make things happen. You can, too. You have a wealth of skills you have not yet discovered.

There may have been times when you looked at somebody who received recognition for his or her accomplishments and thought, *I could do that.* The only difference is that they had the confidence to get it out in the public. Maybe you could do parts of what they have done better, or maybe you could do the whole thing better. Maybe you have something special to add. So why are you hiding your talent?

After my first book was published, somebody asked me how I was selling so many books. I replied, "I'm learning how to toot my own horn—something that goes against every grain of my being, but I know I need to. I'm talking about it everywhere—in the hallway, on the sidewalk, in the stairwell, in checkout lines, etc." I had never been good at selling. I was a certified paragliding instructor for several years and never directly sold any equipment. I knew things had to be different with my books—I had to be different.

That does not mean I had to change my personality. We cannot change our personalities, but instead develop different areas.

Your purpose is as individual as you are. You came into this life with the required skills and talents already encoded for you to achieve your purpose. It is a matter of digging through your own personal toolbox to discover them.

If you give yourself permission to feel proud of your accomplishments what are they? Write them down. Be generous. Count even the small things. What strengths do they reveal? Write these down, too. These are the things you will want to capitalize on as you strive for abundance. As you discover other strengths during your journey, you may need to review these as a reminder of your capabilities at some time in the future. You may also want to add to this list. Be savvy about your limitations. Pursue goals that are compatible with your strengths.

People are like snowflakes. No two are absolutely identical. We may share similarities, but our requirements differ for personal fulfillment. If we all wanted the exact same thing in life, it would be pandemonium, with everybody jockeying for position. Despite judgement from others, we have the opportunity to determine and develop our own sense of fulfillment.

I would disagree with anyone who would say that my grandmother did not feel fulfilled through tending the tiny little garden plot in her backyard when compared to a person whose extravagant multi-tiered garden was featured in the Better Homes and Garden Magazine. She loved her garden and was proud of the vegetables and flowers she grew. There is nothing wrong with wanting to be famous, but you may be somebody who thrives devoting yourself to purposeful activities that are wonderful and meaningful regardless of whether or not you receive public recognition.

No matter how ridiculous you think others would perceive it, what makes you proud?

I feel proud when I make a positive difference in people's lives. I love helping people to develop their intuitive ability so they may communicate with their loved ones in spirit, spirit guides and higher self. My connection with my sons and their loved ones is special to me. When I entice unusual birds to my feeders or coax an unhealthy plant to survive and flower, I feel proud. My ability to organize belongings and prioritize tasks also gives me a sense of pride. You have a plethora of skills and talents, too. What are they?

I often tell myself that even though I am common everyday people, I am capable of great things. If you think you are incapable of producing something creative and spectacular, you need to check it out. I wrote three chapters in my first book believing I might never share it with anybody, but that I would never know unless I tried. I have also since discovered I am able to create unique jewelry and beautiful watercolor paintings.

Can you live with never knowing your potential?

What is the worst that could happen, if you try and you are not pleased with the outcome?

Life is not black and white. There are many gray areas. Recognizing these will help to expand your thinking, opening opportunities for creativity.

We have all been creative at one time or another. This may include cooking a dish without following the recipe, building or repairing something with ingenuity, using an unusual solution, creating something artistic or rearranging your home or garage belongings. It is up to you to tap into your imagination to discover your personal mission.

What activities appealed to you when you were a child? Often, these activities are an indication of gifts and talents. Why do people write, paint, build, play music, sing...because it feels good. There is nothing like doing something that feels rewarding. What pleases you?

What excites you now? What could you do to make it a bigger part of your life, or is it time to add something new? It will be important to be flexible during the self-discovery process. Other possibilities may excite you. It is acceptable to change your mind. This is a trial and error process.

One of the great things I have realized about taking a different path than intended is that I have the opportunity to view scenery I would have otherwise missed. I became lost looking for a bookstore I planned to visit to promote my first book. About the time I started to feel frustrated, I drove around a corner and a vista of rolling green hills spread before me that I did not know existed in southern California. It reminded me of the thrill of my first paragliding flight off of a 360' hill and the fun I had as a paragliding instructor helping others to take their first flights. This provided the option of driving there whenever I felt homesick for the grassy knolls of Canada. I would have missed this opportunity, if I had not taken a different route than intended.

If you keep living life the way you are now, what regrets will you have? Which one scares you the most? What is the worst that could happen, if you put it out there and it failed?

Goals are synonymous with planning. You may not initially be aware of the steps you must take to achieve your dream. Research will help you to plan, but other steps will only become apparent enroute.

It is up to you to choose the *what*, but let the universe help you with *how* and *when*. How much longer you are willing to wait to manifest your dreams is up to you. You also need to determine how you will know when you have reached each of your goals.

What will be happening in your life to show that you have arrived and what will you be doing differently?

When you are attempting to design life goals, it may help to look at what other people are doing. What parts of that person's life do you wish were part of your life? How would you do it differently?

Are there steps you need to take to reach your goals? Would it be helpful to collect more information or consult with somebody to find out what is required? Would it be more productive for you to relax and let the universe work its magic?

An acquaintance of mine planned to pay to have several copies of her manuscript printed. She emailed me to ask whether it was important for her to have them double-spaced because this would be expensive when mailing her manuscripts to publishers. Writers must double-space their manuscripts. More importantly, most publishers do not accept unsolicited manuscripts and most agents only want to see the first one to three chapters unless they request more. It is expensive to send out more than three hundred pages unnecessarily. A little bit of research may save you from wasting time and money.

Each step leads to other opportunities, either for added knowledge about what to do or what to avoid for next steps. Leave room for synchronicity and if developments along the way reveal a better path, be flexible enough to adjust your plan of action.

This is when it becomes important to trust your intuition. If you take one step and it is not the right one, your intuition will pull you in the direction you need to go because you are not alone.

I was watching the Oprah show years ago during an interview with a woman who was 59 years old. She had written her first book and it was a bestseller. I was curious about what she could have written in her novel that would make it a bestseller on her first attempt. I was also thinking about her age. If she could do that at age 59, I could surely do it in my early forties. I bought her book and, after reading it, decided it was the characters that made it compelling. They were unusual and delightful. I could not imagine myself being able to do that. But, I wanted to reach people and I wanted to help people live the lives they wanted to live. What did I have to offer that could make my novel compelling? As mentioned previously, in counseling it is the questions that create change. I decided I would have the main character become involved in counseling and the reader would benefit from the questions asked by the counselor.

Like many things, however, goals are not static. The novel was initially called *A New Beginning*, but the characters took on lives of their own. The next thing I knew, one of the main character's neighbors was teaching her how to share healing energy, which introduces the reader to the process. I ended up renaming the book, *Time To Heal*. The title is a play on words in that it is a story about a woman who is healing while she rebuilds her life and develops self-awareness. In the process, she discovers her spirituality through embracing nature and sharing healing energy.

You must be open to changing your mind or discovering nuances that will cause you to veer off in other directions. Otherwise, you will feel trapped by your goals and they will no longer be a good fit for you.

It becomes an exciting, but informed journey. You can choose or you can let life choose for you. Either way, it is your decision.

> *Like a train that pulls slowly out of the station,*
> *it will gain momentum. You are the conductor.*

If you are serious, commit yourself to your goals by investing your time and money. When I first started writing *Time To Heal*, I hand-wrote notes in my car during my noon hour each day. I later typed the notes on my computer when I returned home.

One day, my previous husband commented, "It looks like you're taking writing seriously. I think we should invest in a laptop computer for you." It saved me a great deal of time and effort once I was able to type my book directly onto a laptop.

One of my grandmother's favorite sayings was, "What goes around comes around." If you mow people over in the pursuit of your goals, you cannot truly experience abundance in its full sense. To achieve a life of abundance involves all of the areas, including ethics. Make sure your behavior is compatible with your values.

What have you wanted to try, but have not because you were afraid you would be incapable or thought you could not afford or did not have the time? If you do not know what your gifts and talents are, ask someone. You might be surprised by the answer.

My twin sister did not know she was artistic. She had not even experimented with drawing, painting or crafts. Karen, however, broke her ankle. During one of her bouts of boredom sitting with her leg elevated, she decided to doodle on her cast. She painted a delightful birdhouse. Karen wondered if she was capable of more, but did not want to invest too much until she experimented a little. She painted a lighthouse on a wooden plaque. Painting became the highlight of her life. She is the artist who painted the original covers of two of my books, *Make It Happen!* and *Messages of Hope and Healing.* She has also discovered she has talent for silk painting and has painted many beautiful silk scarves and paintings.

Some of us do not have enough self-confidence to comfortably pursue our dreams, so we take an easier route. It is not easier, though, because it feels much better when you are on the path to your dreams than when you are not. Life feels exciting and the personal fit is better.

This also comes with lots of fear because most of us experience strong fear of failure or success and self-doubt. Poor self-esteem does not mean you cannot have your dreams and reach your goals. Self-confidence is something that is not achieved overnight, but is built in small steps.

Nothing contributes more to feelings of self worth than following your dreams. Each and every time you sell yourself short, it is an attack on your self-esteem. It may be time to set out and let your dreams happen.

If you feel your energy and motivation waning, focus on raising your vibration level. Remind yourself of the reasons for what you are doing, recall successes and encouragement you have received, do something small that will guarantee success, or connect with somebody you can count on for reassurance. Let them know in advance that this is what you need.

The first day I set out to sell *Time To Heal* in the large office building where I worked, I encountered a group of people I perceived as rejecting. Not only were they not interested in my book, but they seemed perturbed that I had even offered to show them a copy. I backed out of the room and headed down the hallway to a group of people who had made it clear that they wanted to see my book once it was published. Some of them had even indicated they would probably buy a copy. I was warmly received and sold a few copies, which gave me the confidence to approach the next group of unknowns. Each time my self-esteem and confidence level needed another boost, I approached a group I anticipated would be more receptive. Once fueled with more self-confidence, I approached a riskier situation.

Some people only look like they are filled with self-confidence. During times they are feeling low, they pull up their bootstraps, usually through self-talk.

I tell myself, *I can do it* and recall things I may have done that were similar.

I ask, *What's the worst that can happen?* Often the worst is not that bad. It also helps to pretend you are feeling confident. This keeps your vibration up and your enthusiasm will be infectious. Otherwise, simply present a positive attitude. People will generally respond positively to you.

You may break yourself in slowly and experiment to find your authentic self. At times, hobbies and side interests mushroom and become the focus for earning income. Start with small goals, work hard and ensure that you experience some success. Realize that you are not going to immediately get on your path and continue down that road. As mentioned previously, this is a trial and error process, so your route does not need to be perfect.

There may be things you need to know for yourself. Give yourself permission to resolve that tension. Find out whether or not this is what you want.

> *If it does not happen, it was not meant to be.*
> *There is a better opportunity coming up.*

At times, you will make a change and it will not work out the way you had anticipated. This is not a sign of failure. There may be aspects of this change that you like and some you do not. All experience is good because it develops self-awareness. You are now clearer about what you do and do not want.

The road to happiness is not a straight line. You will find that you take two steps forward and one step backward. Expect it and it will not get you as down as it might otherwise. Visualize what you want.

When things do not go as you had hoped, avoid denying your feelings. Nurture yourself. Acknowledge what you learned from the situation and then plan what to do next to get on track.

It is a rare situation where we can hang onto the familiar while seeking out the new. There is only so much room in our lives and often we have to take the bull by the horns, make a leap of faith and cut ties with the familiar. For example, there are some situations where you can keep your full-time job and meanwhile seek part-time education or employment in another area. However, this may run you into the ground and remaining in a job that you have outgrown may wear you down. If moving in this direction excites you and feels good, though, you may need to do it.

Sometimes, it is difficult to make the changes you want without disrupting other areas that are going well. This is when prioritizing becomes essential. Do you want this change enough to give up something else? It will be up to you to determine the level of inconvenience with which you are able to live to reach your goal and, if you have a family, the level of sacrifices you will need them to make to join you in your dream. Due to family and financial obligations, you may have to gradually move into a different field.

You may also find that making change in one area makes you more aware of the need for change in another area.

My first husband and I lived in a small two-bedroom home. When our second child was born, the stress in the house escalated with our two sons sharing a bedroom and constantly waking each other. We moved into a larger home to accommodate our growing family. I loved the spaciousness of our new house and found the additional bedrooms greatly contributed to a peaceful night's sleep, but soon discovered that I was isolated in the new neighborhood. This made me painfully aware of the distance in our marital relationship.

Make the best of a difficult situation, rather than fighting it. Consider this as an opportunity for challenge and do your best to handle it masterfully. It will give you peace of mind and pride. If you are doing something you do not want to do, change your attitude and make it enjoyable or stop doing it.

One of my first jobs was a clerical position where I used a typewriter to type 75 to 100 similar letters each day. I did this job for over one year. The initial challenge involved completing that many letters in a day and teaching the fourteen staff acceptable methods of dictation using a dictaphone machine. The job soon became tedious. I made the work more enjoyable by focusing on developing positive relationships with the staff and competing with myself to see how many letters I could type in a row without any errors and erasures. When that no longer worked for me, I changed jobs.

You will not enjoy the entire journey. Part of what you do to reach your dream will feel great and other parts will be a tolerance test, but you have to get through one to get to the other. You may be tempted to give up, but try to be persistent.

Pick yourself up one more time than you fall down.

My least favorite part of marketing *Time To Heal* was following up on media kits. I scheduled follow-up phone calls for Tuesday and Wednesday mornings because this is apparently the best time to contact radio and television producers. Calls have to be made within 15 minutes after they are out of the studio booths, or they have typically returned home for the day as many start work in the middle of the night. I tended to dread those two days of the week, but they were necessary and I could not let it slide. If I waited too many days before following up, there was no point in making the call. I had to be organized and planful. I made sure I did a lot of self-talk before making those calls. My idea was often rejected, but I kept plugging because there were times it was accepted.

I cannot over-emphasize the importance of being organized. Organization not only helps you to be in control of your life to make things happen, but it also helps you present yourself better to others. People expect professionals to be organized.

Being organized in an area helps you to be more systematic with associated tasks. My media contacts are filed, as are the selection of items I put in my press kits. When I decide to send them out, I have sample letters to draw on to write a letter and I can look through my media kit file to determine which items are suitable for a particular request. Everything is immediately available and this makes the task less overwhelming. When I do follow-up phone calls, I write the names, phone numbers and best time to call so that all I have to do is pick up the list and make the calls. When it is simplified and organized, you will find you have less tendency to practice avoidance. If you know what your plan is when you awake in the morning, this will make the day appear more manageable.

Being planful may also help you sleep, as you will be less likely to spend the night tossing possible ideas around in your head about what you should accomplish the following day. Write a list, so you won't replay ideas in your mind to ensure you remember them.

The time to think about what is on the list is when you are about to do them, not while you are doing something else or relaxing.

You cannot re-invent the wheel every time you approach a task. It is best to leave things in order, so they are less overwhelming upon your return. When I am writing, I find it helpful to stop writing at a point where I have a creative idea for what to write next. I write a brief comment about my idea, so I remember it when I return.

You never know when a creative idea will hit you and if you think it is so great you will never forget it, you may be mistaken. It is better to write down your thoughts, so you may deliberately forget them. It is helpful to carry a pen and paper, so that you don't keep running ideas in your mind to remember them. Otherwise, this interferes with surfacing of other creative ideas.

Some people find it difficult to accept that I don't plan leisure activities during my work hours. When I am working at home, I can find enough to distract myself, without permitting others to pull me away. Plan when you will work on your goals and take a break. You will be much more productive and achieve success sooner. If you are going to take time off, take it off.

Keep work and leisure time separate.

Even if you are going on a working holiday, ensure that you keep a division between leisure time and work by scheduling each at different times of the day or on different days.

Priorities

A teacher asked a student to fill a large jar with golf balls. He asked the class if the jar was full and they agreed it was. He added a bunch of pebbles and shook the jar until they rolled between the golf balls. The students again said the jar was full. He poured in a small bag of sand, which sifted into the empty spaces, and told his students the following:

"The jar is your life. The golf balls represent the important things, such as family, children, health, friends and your passions—all the things that are essential to a fulfilling life. The pebbles represent the other things that count, such as your job, house and car. The small stuff is the sand."

"If you put the sand in first, there is no room for the important things and the things that count. It is the same in your life. If you devote your time and energy to the small stuff, there is no room left for the things that really matter. Set aside time for the things that are necessary for your happiness. Spend time with your children and loved ones. Take care of your health. Enjoy life. Chores can wait. It's all about having priorities. Everything else is just sand."

What time of the day tends to be the most productive for you? Use this time of day to accomplish the things that matter most. Schedule relaxation and less demanding activities for the times of day when your performance tends to be less optimal. Do the things that matter most first. Otherwise, you will run out of time. Be practical. Plan a realistic schedule, so you will not have to operate at a frenetic pace.

It is important to maintain focus. There will be things and people that will try to interrupt you. Schedule breaks for yourself. In the meantime, don't let other things distract you unless it is an opportunity that will help you reach your goal.

You cannot enjoy the rainbow to your dreams,
if you are constantly feeling stressed.

Once you achieve a goal, celebrate and revel in it, but follow up with another one. The highest highs are followed by the lowest lows. It is important to tackle another one to keep your vibration high.

Be careful with whom you share your dreams. If they are not open-minded and supportive, you may become discouraged before you have a chance to get things off the ground.

There will be people who will discourage you—even those who have your best interests at heart. My mother often becomes cautious when I am excited about my dreams because she is afraid I will be disappointed.

Some people believe if you set your expectations too high, you set yourself up for failure. Others are fearful that change in your life will create change in their lives. Some may worry that, if you succeed at your dreams they will also be expected to. Still, others will be afraid that you will surpass their level of success and abandon them. Keep this in mind when you encounter resistance to your ideas, so you do not assume there is something wrong with them.

Dream just past what you think is realistic.
It will be a more accurate measure of what you are capable.

There is no reason in the world that you cannot be as successful or more successful than anybody else could. Self-talk is imperative.

Tell yourself, *I can do this. I have a talent that will benefit others. I will be doing people a favor through sharing my gift.*

If there are lots of people with a similar gift or talent, have faith in abundance. There are more than enough people wanting what you provide to enable you and the others to prosper. Be generous within reason in the confidence that what goes around truly comes around.

I believe that confidence is more than half of the battle. I had less than 24 hours notice for my first television interview. I used self-talk and preparation to help me. I made sure I wrote notes and rehearsed the topic.

Typically, when I am about to do something overwhelming I say to myself, *I'm just little.* This is my way of saying I am normal everyday people, but I am meanwhile telling myself, *Everybody is normal everyday people. Some just have more practice at this. But, you can do it.* I could visualize myself in the studio, which made it seem more possible. I told myself to pretend I was having tea with a friend and answer the questions.

The anchor asked questions I had not expected—she had done her homework. Even though I had not specifically rehearsed this information, the fact that I had prepared as well as I could and the time I spent with positive self-talk helped me to go in feeling relatively confident. This enabled me to respond intelligently.

The next time I was interviewed on television was more than six months later. I was ill with the flu and could hardly talk without breaking into bouts of coughing. I vowed I would be well enough in time to get through the interview, but I had less than three days to make it happen.

I told myself, *I can do this without coughing. I have done this before. It wasn't so hard. All you have to do is answer the questions. Yes, I can do this.* Again, I could see myself in the studio. I could imagine what it would smell and look like. I made myself familiar with the material and set out bright-eyed and bushy-tailed. I was totally engaged in the interview and my illness seemed to suspend for the duration.

Before each of those interviews, I arrived early enough to ground and run energy to calm myself. I did a mock-up visualization, complete with me feeling proud and telling friends and family how well the interview went. This technique will be described later in this book.

What do you say to yourself to keep your spirits up? As mentioned earlier, if you do not feel confident you may find it helpful to pretend that you are, but present yourself as modestly confident rather than arrogant.

At times, when I was about to sit down to write my first book, I felt so overwhelmed, I did not even want to start. On those occasions, I gave myself permission to write only one sentence. Usually, that was not too painful, so I decided to write one more sentence. Often, I felt I might as well finish the paragraph. If that was bearable, I wrote one more paragraph. Sometimes, I became so carried away I was off and running.

Do not beat yourself up, though, for not accomplishing things that stress you. Accept it as fact. Give yourself permission to do something small. If you are able to encourage yourself to do one more small task, do so. If not, let it go for now. This is a start and is in itself commendable.

Sometimes, you will not want to do something with a vengeance, so you should not. Go for a positive procrastination activity. It is a great way to get things done that you do not want to do. Sometimes you will feel so good about your accomplishment that it will enable you to tackle the *monster* task.

Or maybe give yourself permission to take time off.
Savor and enjoy it.

Ten

Make It Happen!

It is important to make a plan and re-evaluate it on a constant basis. Make sure you are on the right track by asking yourself questions. *How does this feel? What are the most important things to me? Is this what this goal will bring me? Is this working, or do I need to try something else?* Be sure you give it enough time, though. Maybe it is working and is not yet obvious.

You can either keep living the way you are, or you can do something different—something that scares you, but at least you are making it happen.

When you have a craving, nothing works as a substitute. You need the real thing. Your life goals need to be like cravings. You want them so bad you can taste them and nothing else will do. It is time to tune into your intuition. Listen to your heart, get in touch with your passion and dreams. It is a good idea to notice what makes your heart beat faster.

What does it look like? Where would you need to be? Who would you like to share your dream with? What steps do you need to take to make it happen? If you don't know, what ideas do you have about where you could go to find out? Is there anyone you know who could help you brainstorm?

One of my goals involved completing a significant cross-country paragliding flight where I would not simply fly over launch and land in the designated landing field below, but would travel a significant distance down the mountain range and land several miles from launch. Due to the extremely short flying season in Canada and the reduced stability of higher performance paragliders in the early years of the sport, Canadian female pilots rarely progressed past the stage of a *sled run*; a flight in which the pilot launches and flies directly to the landing field without achieving altitudes above launch. I wanted to be one of the exceptions.

I chatted with many pilots about their experiences. I asked questions and gained a better understanding of what was required. I went past the stage of *I wish I could have a significant cross-country flight.* to *I really want to...* to *I'm going to...*

I had to create opportunities to help make that happen. For many years, I suffered from a condition that resulted in weakness, stiffness and pain in the muscles, which greatly reduced my physical endurance. Because my son and previous husband could make better use of flying time, I often let them fly. I would traditionally assume responsibility for retrieving the vehicle from launch and driving down the highway to retrieve my son and previous husband from their cross-country flights. I eventually purchased a paraglider with lighter brake pressure that would require less physical endurance and, therefore, enable me to fly further. Although I had had several small cross-country flights, I wanted to fly far enough to demonstrate to myself and others that I was skilled enough to fly a significant distance. My family recognized my ambivalence. It was up to me to take a stand.

I reached the point where I wanted that flight so bad that I could almost taste it. My previous husband and I traveled to different sites and I became accustomed to paragliding in different conditions. Then, we visited our favorite paragliding launch in Golden, British Columbia in Canada and stayed in the community campground for one month. We drove up to launch whenever the conditions looked flyable and I launched whenever the conditions were suitable.

To travel cross-country with a paraglider in Golden, the pilot glides from mountain peak to mountain peak, turning in uplifting air called thermals to gain sufficient altitude to enable him to glide further in order to achieve distance flights. There is a significant valley gap shortly after leaving the Golden launch. The launch altitude is 6,370 feet ASL (Above Sea Level). Pilots flying the Golden site should reach a minimum altitude of 10,000 feet ASL prior to attempting to fly across the gap. Otherwise, they lose so much altitude that they are forced to fly out and land in one of the fields in front of the mountain range.

I had imagined myself on that flight many times. I could see myself circling and climbing up in thermals to the bottoms of the clouds and then gliding all the way past the gap crossing. My goal was to reach Harrogate landing field at a distance of 44 kilometers (25 miles). I had envisioned the landing field and how I would recognize it from the air. Even though I had been there several times, I had only seen it from the ground. To avoid dehydration, I ensured I had enough water with me every time I launched. I persisted and practiced thermaling until the timing was right.

On one particular day, I launched first. My variometer was cheerfully beeping away to let me know whenever I was in uplifting air. My previous husband and a female pilot visiting from Vancouver launched after me. I circled and circled, all the while keeping an eye on the altitude reading of my variometer.

It read 7,000 feet ASL, then 8,000, then 9,000. I was almost at the required 10,000 feet and I was thinking, *Today's going to be the day. I'm going to do it today.*

The other female pilot came on the radio and said, "Look over to the west."

There was a storm front approaching and we had to get on the ground as quickly as possible. I was extremely disappointed.

A few days later, I launched and after an hour of flying around, I had not managed to gain sufficient altitude to cross the gap so I flew out to land. I hitched a ride back up to launch with the idea of either re-launching or retrieving our truck left on launch. Surprisingly, I managed to reach my previous husband on our two-way radio. He was typically down range somewhere, but on this particular day he was at the RV. I did not have to hurry back to let our dog out. He had the motorbike and offered to ride up to launch to retrieve the truck. That left me free to fly. Talk about synchronicity! Pilots were circling above launch, so I could see there were thermaling conditions.

It felt like it was now or never. Everything was in place. All I needed was the fortitude to go for it.

I put on my flying gear, spread out my paraglider and checked my lines with my stomach churning the entire time. I kept reminding myself that getting ready did not mean I had to launch, if I did not feel comfortable.

I commented to a fellow pilot standing nearby, "I wish I didn't feel so anxious on launch."

He said, "Yes, but once you're in the air you always feel much better."

This was all the reassurance I needed. I launched into the next thermal coming up the launch front. I snagged a thermal going up at a rate of more than 1,000 feet per minute. I kept turning until I had climbed out above the rest of the pilots at launch. By the time I reached the gap, I was more than 11,000 feet ASL. I was tickled pink when I made it across the gap. The entire flight was exciting and challenging, as I sought thermal after thermal, rode them up and flew down the range. I was ecstatic once I spotted Harrogate landing field.

I had so much altitude that I was at 5,000 feet over the Harrogate landing field. My son and previous husband later told me that at that altitude I could have easily glided onto Spillimacheen, a small town several miles further down the range. It would have required less physical endurance because I could have used up most of the altitude gliding instead of having to pull a toggle to keep turning in non-lifting air over the Harrogate landing field to lose altitude. But, I had set a manageable task. I knew there was a store, restroom and phone booth available. Those factors, plus familiarity with the landing area, were important for my comfort level for my first significant cross-country flight. Would I have set out that day, if I had not pre-planned to land at Harrogate and had left my expectations open? I do not know, but I sure felt proud when I set down in that field.

When I returned to the campground, I excitedly shared the story of my accomplishment with some of the other females. I later discovered that one of them had flown to Harrogate and landed one field further. When I asked why she did not tell me, she shared that because of my level of excitement she had not wanted to rain on my parade. That was kind, but how could her success diminish my feelings of pride? My accomplishment was personally impressive regardless of her performance. Several of the men had flown flights well over 100 kilometers (62 miles) and Chris Muller, one of the more accomplished male pilots, had flown 240 kilometers (150 miles) that day, but I did not compare myself to them, either.

In order to achieve your goals, it is important that you visualize yourself achieving them. You must have the desire, be clear on the target and make a plan to get you there.

Think to yourself, *I will have that. I really want it and I trust that it will come to me.*

Choose goals that are manageable. There is always the possibility of extending your goal, as you create other opportunities and develop self-confidence.

You need to feel it, breathe it, see it
and almost touch it to help it happen

Passion will help motivate you. Believe in yourself and your ability to make it happen. You can do it. Take the first step!

Visualization

Visualization can often help you achieve your goals. Positive energy accompanies visual images we send out into the universe and attracts more of the same. It is a good idea to use mock-ups to help realize your dreams where you create a vision, ask that it be blessed by the universe and send it out to be created field.

Visual images also help you to feel and think the way you will when it happens. These thoughts and feelings raise your vibration, create positive spirals and help you to become a magnet for what you want. This is why it is often helpful when endeavoring to lose weight to put a photo of yourself with a slimmer body onto your fridge door.

Visualization Exercise

Close your eyes and make yourself comfortable.

Pull your spirit and energy into your body.

Place a rose in front of you.

Imagine what will happen when you get what you want.

Place a video of pictures in the rose that show you getting what you want.

Some examples might include being told you received the job you want, you calling or sending emails to family and friends to share the exciting news, and you smiling and confident at your new job.

Imagine how you are dressed, where you are and what you are doing.

Savor the feeling of having achieved this dream.

Now release this rose to the universe to be manifested.

Take some time to write in your journal.

The heart chakra has a huge influence upon your ability to receive. It is essential for the energy to be open and flowing.

Your heart sends out and brings in energy. Love helps to raise your vibration like nothing else can. The more love you experience, the higher your vibration and your greater ability to manifest. You can create a positive spiral simply by loving something or somebody.

When you send out loving thoughts, you attract loving thoughts.

Opening your heart to receive will help you to receive lots of things, including love in your relationships.

Your heart chakra enables you to experience compassion, forgiveness and love. This chakra helps to create harmony in your relationships.

Open Yourself to Receive More in Your Life Exercise

Bring yourself into a meditative state.

Imagine love flowing in and out with each beat of your heart. Love whooshes in, it whooshes out. It whooshes in, it whooshes out.

Think about the people you love most and open your heart wide to receive their love.

Thank the universe for all of the love you have received throughout your life.

Open your heart wide to receive more love.

Write about how this feels in your journal.

Remove Obstacles to Manifest What You Want Exercise

Bring yourself into a meditative state.

Pull your spirit and energy into your body.

Ask what obstacles are interfering with your ability to manifest.

Ask for help to remove them.

Take some time to write in your journal.

Raise your Vibration to Help you to Become a Magnet Exercise

Bring yourself into a meditative state.

Pull your spirit and energy into your body.

Remember a time in your life that you felt absolutely wonderful.

Now magnify that feeling by 1000. How does this feel?

Re-create this feeling for yourself whenever you think of it.

Maintain a high vibration by remaining positive and enthusiastic about life. Make sure you take a leap of faith. There is no need to stay with the comfortable and familiar.

If you have had a difficult past that has significantly affected your self-esteem and self-confidence, do not let this hold you back. Discover what motivates or inspires you. Bring more of this into your life. Take breaks, but keep moving in the direction of your dream. Get ready for big things to happen.

Take an honest look at your career. Is this what you need to do right now? Is this job the best fit for you and do you feel that what you are doing is worthwhile? Are you proud of your vocation? Are you doing something you are excited and passionate about?

Do the important people in your life support you in your dreams and passions? Do they love you for who you are? What could you do to improve the relationships in your life? Are you making sure your needs are met? What do you need to do to improve your support system?

Reach out. Share yourself. Enlist the cooperation of family and friends as you pursue your dreams.

Work to become less judgmental and recognize life lessons as they come along. This will assist you in responding less emotionally to the challenges presented in your interactions with others. Everybody has his own story. There will be people who will disappoint you. They are doing the best they can, considering their own histories and personal resources. It is no more fair to hold this against them than it is to take it personally.

Experiment with leisure time. It is easy to get caught up in the pace of everyday life and forget about the need to nurture the soul. Permit yourself the opportunity to enjoy life. You are deserving and it will help you to become more loving toward others. Self-love is essential in order to love others with no strings attached and no expectations or resentment.

Treat your body well and nurture your soul. Listen to your body, as it lets you know what you need. Spend time alone. Take time to meditate and live for the moment instead of dwelling on the past or focusing on the future. Benefit from universal energy to cleanse yourself and promote spiritual health.

Make sure your home is a sanctuary for you. Free yourself to enjoy life by facilitating the flow of energy, removing the clutter and getting rid of nagging chores.

Notice in which areas of your life you feel fulfilled. Where is your vibration high? What areas need more work?

You must find your own power and use it to express yourself fully—not to the detriment of others, but as salvation for yourself. During your search for self-discovery, be yourself.

Have you taken a detailed inventory of your strengths and interests? Discover your strengths and expound on them.

The best way to raise your sense of self is to get out there. Start small, but get started. Listen to your intuition. Create flow in your life and move with it. Pay attention to the small steps required. Be receptive to changes in direction. Notice each small success. These are the beginnings of bigger things.

Regardless of your mission, do not settle for mediocre. What are you doing to realize your potential? If you set your sights high, you will create an adventure rather than a struggle for yourself.

When you are doing what you contracted for with the universe, life feels meaningful. You have the free will to choose which way you will travel, as there is more than one acceptable route. Be open to using your intuitive insight to guide you to discover your full capability for personal empowerment.

What are the most important things you want to achieve in your life? If life is passing you by, grab a hold and steer it in the direction you want to go. Not doing anything is a decision on your part to not make it happen.

How many positive spirals have you already developed in your life? Are you on your path?

Make a plan, determine the details and be aware of opportunities, as they unfold.

Be open to new possibilities. Believe in yourself and your dreams.

A meaningful life involves quality time with loved ones, appreciation of life itself and doing something for the good of others. It is important to avoid putting all of your eggs in one basket. Develop a well-rounded life, one with a healthy balance between stability and change. Discover your spirituality. Proceed with the confidence that you are not alone.

Truly Blessed

On a beautiful August day several years ago, I was coming home from a long day of classes at Mira Costa College and decided to stop by the ocean in Del Mar to take a swim. I wanted to be refreshed by the ocean water. The events that happened after I got in the water, however, terrified me to the point that I thought jumping into the ocean was going to be the last thing I did before I died.

I jumped into the water with anticipation and no thought to the conditions of the water or the height of the waves. I just wanted to be cleansed by the water's powerful essence. Suddenly, I could no longer swim, as the waves crashed like a tsunami over my head and pulled me out deeper into the ocean until I could no longer touch the bottom. I panicked and screamed, but to no avail. The waves roared viciously over my screams. There was a man in the water less than ten feet away who could not hear or see me. I also saw a lifeguard truck on the shore and flailed my hands, while screaming with vigor and panic. I realized the lifeguard also failed to see me. I felt helpless and fought the waves until I could no longer fight.

As the waves continued to pound me, I screamed loudly—then suddenly, a strange quiet followed by a feeling of peace filled me. I surrendered to whatever was going to happen because I knew it was no longer in my control. I quit struggling and waited to be pulled under the water to go on my journey to the next life. Suddenly, I felt the sand rise beneath my feet and the waves seemed to get smaller and less violent. I felt totally detached from my body, as I stumbled through the water knowing I had to somehow get to the shore. I felt as if I was watching myself drag my exhausted body to the shore. When I got to the shore, I dropped to the sand and closed my eyes. I lay on the shore for what seemed to be hours. When I opened my eyes, my vision was fuzzy. My eyes burned from the salt and the sun. As I focused more, I saw a beautiful little girl with curly blonde hair and blue eyes, who happened to look like me as a child.

She was staring at me, as if to say, *I know what you went through and you are safe.* Her mother grabbed her hand and she turned her head to stare at me with a look of reassurance. I knew at that moment I had seen the face of God and had been blessed.

As I slowly got up to brush myself off and get in my car to go home, I realized no one on the beach but that precious child had seen me that day. I felt as if I was in another dimension. All these years while I had waited to be rescued by someone else, this day taught me that I could rescue myself under any circumstance, if I just believed enough in myself and trusted the power of God within. It was no accident that the little girl on the beach looked like me as a child—for it was my inner child cheering me on to save myself and giving me the courage to keep on living my life. The message to me was that when challenges come my way, it is wise to surrender and let go of the outcome because I am not in control of the outcome. It also taught me that through pain comes many gifts and I know that I am truly blessed.

Holley Kinnear
Encinitas, California

We are all one. Developing positive spirals in one life influences development of positive spirals in the universe due to the way in which we share energy. Personal development of the soul contributes to the common good.

Work with others to develop one consciousness. Could you imagine the harmony, if the entire universe was united? What are you doing to contribute?

Think of your life as a rosebud waiting to blossom. You cannot leave it lying on the ground. You need to pick it up and nourish it before it will bloom.

Make It Happen!

Bibliography

Adrienne, Carol. *The Purpose of Your Life: Finding Your Place in the World Using Synchronicity, Intuition and Uncommon Sense.* New York: Eagle Book, 1998.

Allenbaugh, Eric. *Wake-Up Calls: You Don't Have To Sleepwalk Through Your Life, Love or Career!* New York: Fireside, 1992.

Altea, Rosemary. *You Own The Power: Stories and Exercises to Inspire and Unleash the Force Within.* New York: Eagle Brook, 2000.

Ban Breathnach, Sarah. *Simple Abundance: A Daybook of Comfort and Joy.* New York, 1995.

Browne, Sylvia. *Conversations With The Other Side.* Carlsbad, California: Hay House, Inc., 2002.

Carter-Scott, Cherie. *If Success Is a Game, These Are the Rules: Ten Rules for a Fulfilling Life.* New York: Broadway Books, 2000.

Chandler, Steve. *100 Ways To Motivate Yourself: Change Your Life Forever.* New Jersey: Career Press, 1996.

Dyer, Wayne. *The Sky's the Limit.* New York: Simon And Schuster, 1980.

Grabhorn, Lynn. *Excuse Me Your Life Is Waiting: the astonishing power of feelings.* Virginia: Hampton Roads Publishing Company, Inc., 2000.

Gray, John. *How to Get What You Want and Want What You Have.* NewYork: HarperCollins Publishers, Inc. 1999

Gurley Brown, Helen. *Having It All.* New York: Simon and Schuster/Linden Press, 1982.

Hansen, Mark Victor and Nichols, Barbara. Out of the Blue...:Delight Comes into Our Lives. New York: HarperCollins Publishers, Inc., 1996.

Leider, Richard J. and Shapiro, David A. *Repacking Your Bags: Lighten Your Load for the Rest of Your Life*. California: Berrett-Koehler Publishers, Inc., 1995.

Mark, Barbara and Griswold, Trudy. *Angelspeake: How To Talk With Your Angels*. New York: Simon & Schuster, 1995.

McGraw, Phillip C. Life Strategies: *Doing What Works, Doing What Matters*. New York: Hyperion Publishing, 1999.

McGraw, Phillip C. Self Matters: Creating Your Life from the Inside Out. New York: Simon & Schuster Source, 2001.

Moore, Thomas. *Care of the Soul: A Guide for Cultivating Depth and Sacredness in Everyday Life*. New York: HarperCollins, 1992.

Morris, Tom. *True Success: A New Philosophy of Excellence*. New York: Berkley Books, 1994.

Patent, Arnold M. *You Can Have it All*. Oregon: Beyond Words Publishing, Inc., 1995.

Pitino, Rick. *Success Is A Choice: Ten Steps to Overachieving in Business and Life*. New York: Broadway Books, 1997.

Redfield, James. *The Celestine Prophecy*. New York: Warner Books, Inc, 1993.

Richardson, Cheryl. *Life Makeovers: 52 Practical and Inspiring Ways to Improve your Life One Week at a Time*. New York: Broadway Books, 2000.

Sher, Barbara. *Live the Life You Love*. New York: Dell Publishing, 1996.

Vedral, Joyce F. *Look In, Look Up, Look Out: Be the Person You Were Meant To Be*. New York: Warner Books, Inc., 1996.

Wholey, Dennis. *The Miracle of Change: The Path to Self-Discovery and Spiritual Growth*. New York: Pocket Books, 1997.

Wieder, Marcia. *Making Your Dreams Come True*. New York: Random House/Harmony Books, 1993.

Zukav, Gary. *The Seat of the Soul*. New York: Fireside, 1989.

www.ingramcontent.com/pod-product-compliance
Lightning Source LLC
LaVergne TN
LVHW051511080426
835509LV00017B/2023